KEITH IR

THE RELUCTANT SOLDIER:

TWO YEARS OUT

Figure 1. Royal Electrical and Mechanical Engineers Insignia.

Figure 2. The Worcestershire Regiment.

THE RELUCTANT SOLDIER

TWO YEARS OUT

KEITH IRVING

R.E.M.E

(ROYAL ELECTRICAL AND MECHANICAL ENGINEERS)

1954 to 1956

Paperback ISBN: 9798398243048

First paperback edition June 2023

Foreword by Jennifer Irving
Edited by David-Jack Fletcher of Chainsaw Editing
Cover design by Jennifer Irving
Layout by David-Jack Fletcher of Chainsaw Editing
Photographs by Keith Irving
Additional illustrations by Jennifer Irving

Disclaimer: The characters in this book are the work of memory to the best of the author's ability. Any divergence contrary to other accounts of the same events is unintentional and the product of the author's experience and recollection.

Dedicated to my family

FOREWORD

As a historian, I have long been captivated by the power of personal stories and their invaluable contribution to our understanding of historical events. They offer a window into the lives of ordinary individuals who have experienced extraordinary times. Today, as I have the privilege of writing this foreword for the memoir of my grandfather, Keith Irving, I am reminded of that profound importance of family histories.

Keith was conscripted into national service in Britain during the mid-1950s. Like many, he witnessed and experienced an era that shaped the course of countless lives. His memoir, written two decades ago, illuminates a chapter of history that is often overshadowed by the tumultuous aftermath of World War Two. It sheds light on the personal memories, challenges, and triumphs of those who came of age during a transformative period in history.

In delving into Keith's narrative, we embark on a journey through his recollections, where we gain a deeper understanding of the human experiences that were woven into the fabric of post-war Britain. It is through the lens of personal accounts, that we are provided a bridge between generations, enabling us to connect with the past and appreciate the struggles and resilience of those who came before us.

Moreover, this memoir holds a special significance as we celebrate my grandfather's 90th birthday. It not only honors his life but also allows us to treasure his legacy of knowledge, a precious gift that we can pass on to future generations. A gift many families aren't able to obtain. The preservation of personal histories is an act of love, a testament to our commitment to understand where we come from and to illuminate the paths we traverse.

As we turn the pages of this memoir, we are reminded of the importance of cherishing and recording our own family histories. We offer our descendants a deeper connection to their roots and empower them with the wisdom and lessons of those who came before. Through family histories, we shape our collective narrative, embracing the diverse voices that have shaped our shared existence. I invite you to embark on this journey through my grandfather Keith's experiences in national service and the years that bordered it.

Thank you Grandda for sharing with us, your family, and the world, especially when so many stories get lost to time. It may not be the story of extraordinary feats, but that is what makes it so wonderful and relatable. We love you very much.

Jennifer Irving, Ph.D., Granddaughter of Keith Irving

Acronyms

L.N.E.R	London and North Eastern Railway
M.T.O.	Motor Transport Officer
N.A.A.F.I.	Navy, Army and Air Force Institutes
N.C.O.s	Non-Commissioned Officers
R.A.F.	Royal Air Force
R.E.M.E.	Royal Electrical and Mechanical Engineers
R.S.A.	Returned Service's Associations
R.S.M.	Regimental Sergeant Major

AUTHOR'S NOTE

These pages contain my memories of the time that I spent doing my national service in the 1950s. Every serviceman looks back at their time in the forces. Memories of both the good times and the bad, and certainly of times he wouldn't like to see in print.

Aside from the men who served in the Second World War, it is well documented that over two million men served during the time when the national service was in force. I believe reading this book will be of interest to the men and their families. Especially the younger members, who like to hear what the older members were up to in their young days.

To give the reader an insight into how life was lived in those days, I've included a section about my life up to and including the Second World War, then the time leading to my national service. I served with the Royal Electrical and Mechanical Engineers (R.E.M.E) doing my initial training in Honiton in Devon. Most of my service was spent in Germany attached to the Worcestershire Regiment stationed in Iserlohn.

THE RELUCTANT SOLDIER
TWO YEARS OUT

Every now and again, it appears in the newspapers or on the television that a lot of people would like to see the return of the national service. National service meant all males at the age of eighteen had to serve two years in either the Army, Navy or Air Force.

There were a few exceptions (very few I might add), the main exemption based on medical grounds. Others based on your occupation, such as farm workers and coal miners. There were, of course, conscientious objectors but these people were few and far between and I doubt if there were many who were excused because of their beliefs.

The fact that at varying times people feel that national service would instil some discipline into the youth of today, and my grand-children asking me about the time that I spent in the army, prompted me to look into the archives of my mind to recall the two years I spent doing my national service between October 1954 and October 1956.

As I've already said, the age for receiving your calling up papers was eighteen. But because I was serving my apprenticeship – I usually say 'serving my time', though my wife says it sounds as if I were doing a stretch in prison – it was possible that I could be deferred until my apprenticeship was finished at the age of twenty-one.

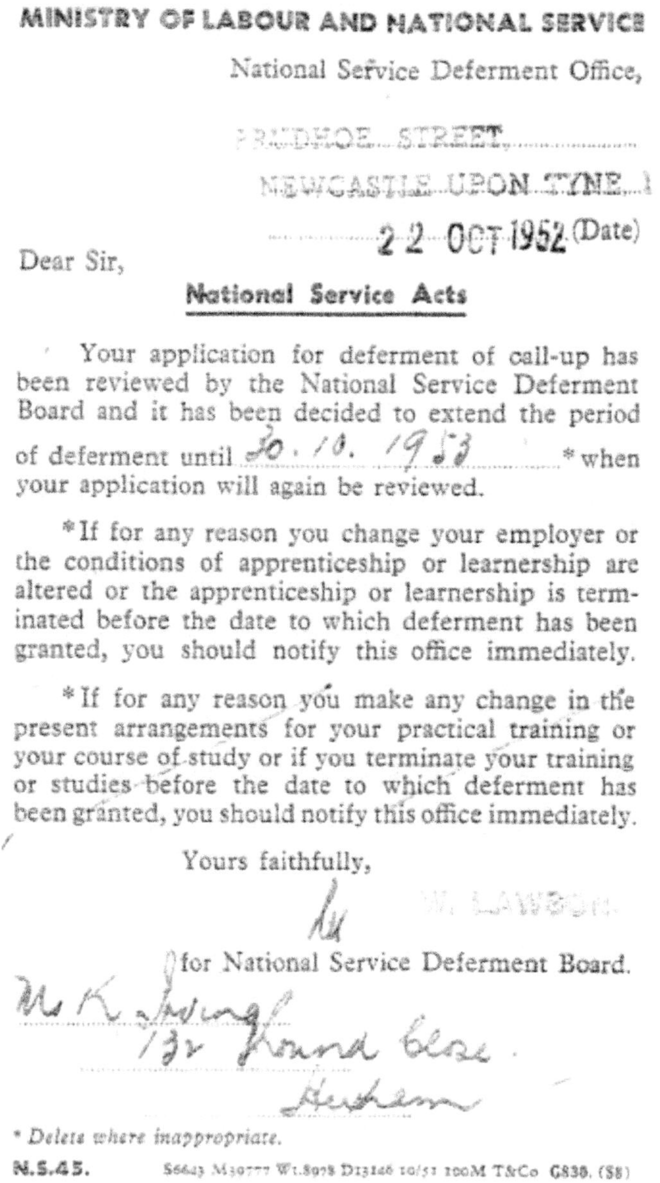

MINISTRY OF LABOUR AND NATIONAL SERVICE

National Service Deferment Office,

PRUDHOE STREET,

NEWCASTLE UPON TYNE 1

22 OCT 1952 (Date)

Dear Sir,

National Service Acts

Your application for deferment of call-up has been reviewed by the National Service Deferment Board and it has been decided to extend the period of deferment until 30.10.1953 *when your application will again be reviewed.

*If for any reason you change your employer or the conditions of apprenticeship or learnership are altered or the apprenticeship or learnership is terminated before the date to which deferment has been granted, you should notify this office immediately.

*If for any reason you make any change in the present arrangements for your practical training or your course of study or if you terminate your training or studies before the date to which deferment has been granted, you should notify this office immediately.

Yours faithfully,

W. LAWSON

for National Service Deferment Board.

Mr K. Young

13 Round Close

Hexham

* *Delete where inappropriate.*

N.S.45. S6643 M30777 Wt.8078 D13146 10/51 100M T&Co G838. (S8)

Figure 3. Ministry of Labour and National Service. 22 October 1952.

I sent off for the necessary papers to see what was involved. On receiving them, everything seemed straight forward, so I filled them in and sent them off. One thing that I had to do was to get someone in a position of authority to sign them but it couldn't be a relative. So, I got the local councillor to sign them, only for them to be returned saying his signature wasn't acceptable as far as they were concerned, and that I would have to get them signed by someone else. They sent me a list of the people who they considered to be suitable.

I was serving my apprenticeship with British Rail as a heavy goods vehicle mechanic and I was a member of the National Union of Railwaymen, so I got the union secretary to sign. I sent them off – thankfully, this time they were accepted – and I would be deferred until I was twenty-one.

Whether it was the best thing to do or not was debatable; a lot of men would go in at eighteen and finish their apprenticeship at the end of their service. I suppose in one way you were just delaying the inevitable, because come what may you would have to do the service, there just wasn't any way out of it. However, that's what I decided to do, but it's a true saying that time marches on and, before I knew where I was, the time had passed and I was coming up to my twenty-first birthday.

A few months before my birthday I received word I would have to go down to Newcastle for a medical. I'm not positive, but it's in the back of my mind that I had to report to a centre in the vicinity of the Haymarket. On the given day I travelled down to Newcastle and reported to reception.

There were a lot of men reporting that day, I was told to go into a cubicle, strip down to my underpants and join the men sitting in the corridor. One chap, after being told the procedure, came out of the cubicle absolutely starkers and proceeded to run down the corridor much to everyone's amusement. However, he was promptly told to go back to the cubicle, put his underpants on and join the rest of us and wait to be called.

After a while you were called and given a thorough examination; much to my surprise I was told I had a slight hearing problem. I must say it was something I hadn't noticed before. But anyway, I had my ears syringed – what a difference it made, I couldn't believe it. I got through all the tests and the examiner was pleased with the results and so I passed. I would receive word in the not-too-distant future when and where I would have to report.

As I was coming to the end of my apprenticeship I received word from British Rail that I would be on three months' notice. So, from the twenty-first of August 1954 I would have three months to apply for a position in the railway network. In fact, it never got to that as I was called up before the three months expired. The law at that time stated that if you were employed when you were called up, the firm would have to offer you a job at the end of your service.

After my medical I would be looking every day for a letter to tell me where I would have to report. But as the days went by with no sign I just forgot about it. I was playing football for a local team at the time and I was enjoying that. I was approached by another team wanting me to play for them, but I had to tell them that I would be going into the army before too long so it wouldn't be worth my while changing.

I knew a couple of other chaps who were due to be called up at the same time as me. So, when we met we would be able to compare notes but they weren't hearing anything either. One day I went into the house. There was no one else in at the time, so it was a while before I noticed a letter propped up on the side board. It looked very official and I thought to myself this is the one that I've been waiting for.

Lo and behold it was my calling up papers telling me where and when I had to report for duty. I had to report to Honiton in Devon on the fourth of October 1954 and I would be joining the R.E.M.E.

CHAPTER ONE

At this point I would like to digress. The reason being that I think it would be a good idea to give you, the reader, an idea of how life was being lived at the time. So, you can compare with how it's being lived today. This was triggered by a remark made by one of my grandsons. He was asking how far I could go back in time. What could I remember about my early days? This set me thinking, and so I decided I would like to include a section about my early years. As well as a section to cover the time after I'd finished national service.

I was born in a small village in County Durham called Medomsley, a village about three miles from Consett. Consett was a well-known town noted for the big ironworks situated there, something which no longer exists. I remember that during the war, the Germans were always trying to bomb it. This wasn't a surprise considering the furnaces could be seen from villages away. At that time, it was a big employer in the town and it must have been a big blow to the town when it was closed down; a sign of the times.

Medomsley was my mother's home village, and I'm sure that was the reason for me being born there, as my mother's family still lived in the village. I'm sure that my grandmother would have played a big part in bringing me into the world. Although, I did hear years later that one of the women in the village was always called upon to assist at the births. There was always a good community spirit in these villages.

At the bottom of Medomsley was the coal mine, so most of the men were employed in what was called 'the pit'. In those days they didn't have the facilities that they do today. They would finish their shift and arrive home covered in coal dust. There weren't any showers, they would have to wash in a bathtub in front of the fire. My grandmother had an outside toilet which was very much the norm in those days.

I can still remember my great grandmother who lived about a hundred yards away. For the benefit of anyone who can remember Medomsley at that time, beside the butcher's shop. My great grandfather – I can't remember but I was often told the story – had a horse and cart and would do jobs around the area.

My great aunt lived next door to my grandmother and as I grew older she would often take me to the cinema at Leadgate; something I enjoyed as she was good to me. One thing that sticks in my mind about her was that she had a ferret. It had belonged to my uncle, but it bit him, so he gave it to my great aunt. She would buy rabbits for it, and as it knew where it was well off, it never bit her. Leadgate had a couple of pubs and also, I suppose, what we would call now, a couple of corner shops.

Also, in the village was a big co-operative store, which had all the different departments, and above these was a big hall where all the weddings and other functions took place. In those days the Co-Op played a large part in people's lives.

You would have a number; this number would be taken after every purchase and from this a dividend would be paid every so often. This was the way that the women of the house could manage to get a few pounds together. A lot of the women's savings would be down to the Co-Op dividend, they would always be looking forward to divi day.

Although I was born in Medomsley, I was raised in Hexham in Northumberland, which was my father's hometown. But most of my school holidays would be spent in Medomsley. As I grew older my mother would put me onto Robson's bus; this was a Slaley firm (another village southeast of Hexham) that ran the bus service between Hexham and Consett. My grandmother would meet me off the bus and I would spend the school holidays with her.

One of the big perks of staying with my grandmother was the fact that I had a lot of relations in the area, which meant that I would get a penny or two from each one. By the end of the holidays I could have saved a tidy sum. Believe it or not, over the time I could have got together two shillings – ten pence in today's currency – so I would be going home rich!

Another thing about Medomsley was the big church, which was a popular place for weddings. On a wedding day all the kids of the village would gather there as the father of the bride would throw out a handful of coins as the wedding car was leaving. As you can imagine, there would be a mad scramble to see how much you could pick up, and it wasn't only the kids either.

During World War II, I was on holiday in Medomsley, when a bomb dropped just a few hundred yards from my grandmother's house.

The next day she took me up to see what damage had been caused, fortunately it had missed the houses and landed in a field, where it made a big crater. I can only imagine that it had been looking for the Consett Ironworks and finished up a bit wide of the mark. But whatever they were looking for it was too close for comfort for me, so I decided that discretion was the better part of valour and so I went off home the next day.

After a few years my grandmother moved to a village a short distance away called The Dene. The old house had no bathroom and an outside toilet, whilst the new house had all mods so it was much better all round for everyone. I really liked The Dene and I spent a lot of enjoyable holidays there.

The village was built in the middle of a lot of farmland. During the summer holidays the farmer would be leading hay from the fields to be stored at the farm. This work was all carried out by horse and cart, so we would spend long days helping the farmer. The hay was all in stacks, and the stack would be pulled onto the trailer, and then we would head off to the farm sitting at the back; the bit that I enjoyed the most. This job would go on for days, and maybe I'm imagining things but the sun would shine every day. Looking back the weather seemed to be more reliable than it is today. Although, it has to be said that Consett could get some big snow falls. The journey across from Hexham on the bus could be pretty hairy at times with the state of the roads.

CHAPTER TWO

Hexham, my home town, is situated very close to the River Tyne, it is a very nice market town about eighteen miles west of Newcastle and known because of its position as the Heart of England. In the centre of town is the market square which is dominated by the Abbey.

The main event of the week would be the Tuesday market when it would be filled with stalls selling all sorts of goods. It was also a meeting place where you would get together with your mates before heading off to wherever you were going that night. One of the things that I can recall, and is clear in my mind, was the birth of my youngest brother at home when I was five. At that time, we were living in a one-bedroom house. There were four houses on the block: two on the street, and two around the back.

So, with my Mother and Father and three children (myself and two younger brothers) there wasn't a lot of room. My mother would often be at the council's housing office trying to persuade them to give us a council house. But with everyone in the same boat it was a long, slow process moving up the list. You had to fetch water from a tap at the back of the houses, also round the back was the outside toilet, the coal house, and the wash house.

Every Monday, my mother would be up early to get the fire going in the wash house, ready for her to carry out the weekly wash. This would be a full day's work and it would be late in the afternoon before she would be finished. There were no machines in those days, everything would be done by hand. Every house in the block would have a share in the wash house so everyone would have to stick to their allotted day.

The outside toilet was a problem at times as one of the neighbour's kids had a bad habit of locking the door while you were inside. This led to a lot of strife between his mother and mine, to say that they weren't on the best of terms was putting it mildly. However, the funny thing was that years later they were in the same club (probably the over sixties) and on the committee, and much to the amusement of myself and my two brothers they were the best of pals – not something you could ever have imagined in our young days.

One good thing, though, was that there was a path at the side of the house, and on the other side was the wall of the blacksmith's shop so it made an ideal cricket pitch, and many a happy hour was spent practising cricket.

The blacksmith's shop held a great fascination, as we would see the horses coming in to be shod. We would be able to watch the blacksmith in action, the blacksmith being a very busy man. There were plenty of horses around in those days.

Opposite the house there was this huge orchard full of apple and pear trees. When the fruit was ripe we would be so sick eating fruit we would have fruit fights and throw it at one another. I'm sure that was an awful waste, but because of the war no one was taking any interest in the orchard. You couldn't eat it all, so we spent some happy times throwing it at one another.

Now after all these years this area is covered with garages, super markets, and other businesses. But part of it is a garden centre; at least it still has some connection with the past.

I do remember there being a small orchard along the road, which was full of pear trees. We used to call the pears Green Jacks. I'm sure they'll have a different name, but I don't know what it is. You would know them by their shape and they were very sweet.

The owner of the orchard kept a watchful eye on them, so if you wanted any you would have to go to him and buy them. He would sell you the pears for a penny or tuppence, you would get a lot and there were no plastic bags in those days. So, you would put your jersey inside your trousers and stuff the pears inside, then you would be off home looking like a wee barrel – happy days!

In those days there was very little traffic on the road, in fact the coke works which was just along the road was fed by horse and cart from the railway station. Coke being a coal-based fuel which was popular up until the 1960s when it was replaced by natural gas. The horses would be back and forth all day long. Nearly everyone on the street had an allotment so there was always plenty of manure, and everyone would be out with their buckets and spades. At that time, we would have double summer time, changing the clocks back two hours so that we would have really long days.

The games we used to play at that time were girds, which was a metal ring that you would hit with a stick running along the road, or you could use a bicycle wheel without a tyre, which did the same job.

Nowadays if you see a kerb you'll see a car parked beside it. In my opinion, kerbs were designed so that kids could use them for their proper purpose, and that was for having a game of marbles. There was no traffic on the road so you could play to your heart's content, that is unless a horse came galloping along at thirty miles an hour. Our local shop was at the bottom of Gilesgate bank where you could get any messages that your mother sent for you.

One of the neighbours was a miner, and like a lot of miners he loved his pigeons. He had a loft down the Chines (river gorge) and I loved to go down there and give him a hand. He would race the pigeons, and on a race day he would gather his entries into a basket and we would take them along to the club house at the railway station. The officials would take the entry and put a rubber ring onto the pigeon's leg, then they would be sent off by train to wherever they were facing from.

The races were for varying distances and sometimes they would send them to the continent. He would get word at what time they had been released so we would be down at the loft in good time waiting for their return. On their return they had to fly over the orchard, so you wouldn't see them until the last second as they swooped over the trees and straight into the loft.

All the fanciers had a clock, and when they'd entered the birds the clock would be set by the officials so when the birds arrived home the fancier would take off the rubber ring and put it into the clock. The clock would lock and record the time of the bird's arrival. The neighbour had some good birds so he used to do quite well. I used to look forward to race days.

At this time holidays abroad were unheard of, I was lucky to be able to spend the school holidays with my grandmother. During which was a special day in the year, the day of the Sunday school trip. This involved going along to the railway station where there was a special train laid on to take the Sunday school kids on a trip to the seaside for the day. We would go down to Whitley Bay where a good day would be had by all, a day to remember. Something we all looked forward to.

CHAPTER THREE

About this time my father got his calling up papers for the army in 1939. I remember standing at the bottom of Eastgate when a convoy came past with my father riding a motorbike and sidecar, as they headed off to goodness knows where. There was a big crowd watching for their men folk not knowing when they would see them again. A lot of them no doubt never seeing their loved ones again. This was a time of great uncertainty with the women being left to look after the families. A lot of women worked in the factories and some of them became land army girls; everyone had to pull their weight there was a war on.

The day that war broke out, I was walking along Fore Street with my mother. She was pushing my youngest brother along in a pram. The siren sounded, so we about-turned and headed back home. My mother had to bring the three of us up on her own, it has to be said we were always well looked after.

At this time ration books were issued, which meant everyone was only allowed a certain amount of necessities in the food line per week. This was something that was strictly adhered to – no coupons, no goods. You would also be issued with clothing coupons, rationing went on all through the war years and wasn't finally repealed until the early nineteen-fifties.

At that time, we would have long hot summers with the sun shining every day for weeks on end. The River Tyne was just a few minutes' walk away from home so one of my favourite pastimes was to go down to the river to learn how to swim. There would be a crowd and we would all enjoy the day, we found a big rock just off the river bank. We would jump off and you would have to sink or swim – you would soon learn how to swim. The bigger boys were always around to make sure that you didn't get into any trouble. Tyne Green was a very popular area and still is to this day; very enjoyable walking along the river banks with a lot of families having picnics, and plenty of space for the kids to run around.

In those days your parents didn't have to worry, they knew where you were and who you were with and they knew that no one would bother you (changed days I'm afraid). You enjoyed the simple life, you didn't spend hours in front of a TV screen, or glued to a computer for hours on end. You were outside getting the fresh air and a much healthier life.

Every Easter, our mother would take the three of us to a clothes shop, which was a few miles from Hexham. We would all get a new suit and it would be paid up weekly. My mother didn't get much money but she always made good use of what she did get. Something that I feel has rubbed off on the three of us. The suits would be for Sunday best, we would go to Sunday school so we were always well turned out.

One of the reasons for me including this section is to say a few words about discipline. I'm not saying that we were angels but we were always kept in order by our mother. If you got into trouble at school, you would be punished there, and when your mother found out you would be punished again. That was pretty much the norm for everyone in those days.

If you were off school for any reason, the school board man would turn up at your door to find out the reason why you weren't in school. He would have to go away believing there was a genuine reason for you being off; if not, you would hear more about it. So, I don't imagine there was much truancy in those days.

As far as the three of us were concerned, one of my aunts used to say that if one of us misbehaved my mother would smack the three of us because she didn't like the other two to feel left out. These were the days when children would be seen and not heard, now I'm not saying this was right, I'm just saying that is how it was. I don't think by any stretch of the imagination that being seen and not heard could be applied to the youngsters of today, the pendulum seems to have swung the other way.

I'm old fashioned but I feel that respect and discipline should play a large part in the upbringing of youngsters. It's a debate that goes on and on with plenty of people having ideas but no one sorting the problem.

Once the war started it was blackout time, all the windows in the house would have to be blacked out. A team of wardens would parade the streets, if they saw a sliver of light there would be a rap on the door and you would be told to cover it up. You would be in serious trouble if you failed to act on the warnings that you were given. We were all issued with gas masks and these would have to be carried at all times. Even the babies would be issued with a full body cover and I can remember my mother being shown how to set it up.

We would have the masks at school and when the siren sounded we would all file into the special air raid shelters that had been built in the school playground. During the war I was a pupil at the Sele school in Hexham. In fact, most of the war I was in the infant and junior school there. So, we would spend quite a bit of time in these air raid shelters, the teachers would have their work cut out to try and keep us amused until the all-clear sounded. Then we would all troop back to our classrooms to resume our lessons.

Behind the Abbey there was a lovely park with a band stand in the middle. About Easter time, we would have a fete and one of the highlights would be the kids dancing around the maypole. We would be practising for weeks to make sure that everything was perfect on the day. It was very colourful and surprising the patterns that could be made weaving in and out.

Beside the school was the Sele, this was a big area of grassland with a football pitch at the bottom and a steep hill at the side of the pitch. This hill came into its own in the winter time, when all the sledges would be out as it made a lovely long run. In the summer it would often be used for the fair ground and of course there were always the usual swings, so it was a popular place for families to spend time on the hot summer days. One of the things that we would do at that time was collect rose hips. We would gather these and take them to school where we would be given so many a pound, from there they would be sent off to make rose hip syrup. Another thing that we used to collect at that time was jam jars, we would take them back to the shop and they would give us so much per jar.

From the Sele school, I went to the secondary modern school, which was a lot further from home and meant me walking through the town centre, up Eastgate, cross a footbridge over a ravine, and into the school.

SCHOOL REPORTS

You know how it is when you are looking for something and no matter how hard you try you just can't find it. Invariably what happens is you find something you've forgotten all about. In this case I found these two school reports that my mother must have kept.

The first one is from my time in the Hexham Infants school, part of the Sele school, which was for 1941. The second one is from the secondary modern school in 1947.

Keith Irving

<u>HEXHAM</u>   <u>COUNCIL</u>   <u>INFANTS</u>
           <u>SCHOOL</u>

<u>SUMMER</u> <u>Term</u>   Report
            1941.

Reading $\frac{10}{10}$ Very good.
Arithmetic $\frac{4}{10}$ Poor.
Handwriting $\frac{9}{10}$ Good, careful work.
Composition $\frac{7}{10}$ Fairly good
Dictation $\frac{7}{10}$ Fair.
English Exercises $\frac{8}{10}$ Good.
                 $\frac{45}{60}$

{ Nature
{ Geography   Fairly good.
{ History

{ Needlework   Good, careful work.
{ Handwork

Recitation   Fairly good
Conduct   Very good.

Remarks   Keith tries very hard
indeed with his work and has
shown considerable improvement.

                J. Skeen. Headmistress
            M. Hewitson Class Teacher

Figure 4. Keith Irving's report card. Hexham County Modern

ATHLETICS.

K IRVING   HEXHAM COUNTY MODERN SCHOOL 1947

	Performance.	Attitude.
Physical Training ...	B	F
Games — Football ...	B	L
Games — Hockey ...		
Games — Netball ...		
Games — Tennis ...		
Games — Cricket ...	L	C
Games — Swimming ...		
Games — Rounders ...		
Games — Field Sports	B	A

Attendance ... ... Very Good.

Punctuality ... Very Good.

Participation in School Activities ... A very keen member of the school choir; gives his best always.

Positions of Responsibility held ... ... Team captain

Conduct ... ... Very Good Indeed always. Is most attentive, & helpful.

Additional Remarks An excellent report; thoroughly well deserved; Keith is intelligent works hard, & always gives his best: He is happy at the school.

.... J. Williams .... Form Master/Mistress.
.... J. Hall .... Head Master/Mistress.

This Slip should be signed by the Parent and returned to the Head Master/Mistress.

Figure 5. Keith Irving's Summer Term report card. Hexham Council Infants School. 1941.

The reason for me to include these is not to show off my educational skills, such as they are. But when I looked at them and saw the names of the Headmistress and the Headmaster it brought back memories of the time I spent in their schools.

Miss Skeen was Headmistress of the Infants school, and Mr. Slater the Headmaster of the Secondary school. I remember them both as strict disciplinarians. Especially Mr. Slater, years after you had left school and he had retired, you would meet him in Hexham. He knew every pupil that had ever been in his school by name. So, he would greet you by name and you after all that time would still call him 'sir'.

CHAPTER FOUR

After the war, my father returned home; he had been a cobbler by trade, so he went back to that job. But because he suffered badly from stomach ulcers, and with a lot of standing involved in the work, it wasn't suiting him so he managed to get a job in the Hexham General Hospital. He was very lucky to get a job at all – with all the men returning from the forces and all looking for work, there weren't a lot of jobs available.

Just along the road from where we lived on Haugh Lane there was a community centre, so a lot of the men would spend their days there. I suppose just filling in time until a job would turn up. One of the things that did keep them going to a certain extent was that many of them had allotments. My mother looked after the allotment while my father was in the forces. We had a small greenhouse so we would always have plenty of tomatoes during the season.

My mother would be still going into the council's housing department to keep at them in the hope that we would be allocated a council house. At last, after years of trying, she was successful; we had been allocated a house in Round Close. What a difference – a bathroom and toilet in the house. An added bonus: it was just a couple of minutes' walk to school.

There was a grocer's shop in the marketplace, my mother was a customer there. At that time, you didn't walk around picking what you wanted off the shelves. There was an assistant behind the counter – you would tell her what you wanted, she would get everything together, write them all down, and price them and add it all up. Mental arithmetic was pretty good in those days. One day I was in the shop with my mother, when the manager asked me if I would like a job delivering messages to customers' houses after school. I accepted, and my first job would be as a message boy for Thompson's Red Stamp Stores.

At first, I would load the messages onto a barrow and trundle around the streets with that. Pushing the barrow was a tedious task as I had to cover a wide area and would be heading off in many different directions after school. Places I remember delivering to were the West End, Round Close, Wanless Close, Elvaston down Tyne Green, and numerous other places.

I have to admit that pushing this barrow about wasn't my favourite pastime, especially as other message boys in the town were riding around on message bikes. One benefit I did enjoy was that the customers were often very kind and would give me a tip, which was much appreciated. The Red Stamp Stores was a very busy shop, so I was kept on the move after school.

In the shop, they had an old delivery bike with a basket on the front. It looked a bit of an antique but I wasn't caring what it looked like as long as it saved me from having to push the barrow around. It needed a few repairs but after many attempts I managed to get the manager to have it repaired. I put it into a repair shop and could hardly wait until I got it back. In due course it arrived, so I would fill the basket with orders and off I would go. What a difference – it was like being in seventh heaven! Normally I would just fill the basket, but one day I had a couple of extra boxes for the same area so I stuck them on the top. Off I set, good style cycling down Priestpopple with not a care in the world.

I was heading for Round Close, so at the bottom of Priestpopple I would have to turn right. Which I duly did, but the boxes on the top went straight on. Luckily there wasn't a lot of traffic around in those days so I managed to pick up the messages and put them back into the boxes. Off I went again to make the deliveries.

At the first house I gave the lady of the house the box, she would empty the box and give it back to me. While I was standing at the back door I heard her say to someone, 'You would think these groceries had been thrown into this box'. Little did she know that she wasn't far wrong. For the next couple of days these two customers would be coming into the shop saying that they'd got items they hadn't ordered and some of the items they had ordered were missing. Never mind, it sorted itself out through time thank goodness.

By this time, I was getting to the age that I would be leaving school, but unfortunately, the government decided – in their wisdom – to raise the school leaving age to fifteen. So, this meant that I would have to spend another year in school, which didn't go down very well with me, but there was no way out of it.

During October, we would get a week's holiday from school, which we called 'Tattie Week'. At times during the term we would be allowed to go tattie (potato) picking for half a day. You would be paid two shillings and sixpence for the half day (twelve and a half new pence) by the farmer. It wasn't a job I particularly liked, it was back-breaking. I don't think there were many people that did enjoy it, but at least you got away from the school for half a day. The farmer would pick you up in the morning with his tractor and trailer and then bring you back at lunch time. I was getting near to school-leaving-age and starting to think about what job I would get.

I used to go for my haircuts to the barbers on Back Street, the barber was a friend of my father's and they'd been in the army together. He would say to me, 'When you leave school you can come and work for me'. I'm sure that I would have been treated well and that I would have enjoyed the job. But by that time, I had started to play football and really enjoyed the game. So as Saturday was the barber's busiest day of the week I felt that I couldn't take up the offer.

CHAPTER FIVE

I left school and started to look for a job. One job I was interested in was as a second man on a laundry delivery van. The vans would cover a wide area so you would always be on the move. I think one of the attractions was that you had to carry a money bag slung over your shoulder, which I'm sure made you feel important. However, I never got to take the job as I was offered an apprenticeship with the L.N.E.R. (London and North Eastern Railway) which I decided to accept. I would be based at Hexham railway station, where there was a small workshop. We covered a big area so I was still able to get out and about. The area included Haydon Bridge, Haltwhistle, Brampton, the North Tyne, Stocksfield and over to Consett. I would be serving my apprenticeship as a heavy goods vehicle mechanic.

My first week's wages was one pound, four shillings and sixpence (in today's money vernacular one pound, twenty-two and a half pence), which is laughable when you consider that the minimum wage today is probably four times as much as that for one hour. I liked the job and the people I was working with, so I soon settled in. One of the things I enjoyed about the job was that the railway used to hire out horse boxes.

On the outskirts of Hexham there is a very nice place – National Hunt Racecourse. There would be regular race meetings so three or four of these boxes would attend. The mechanic and I would be on duty in case there were any problems with the boxes. Not that you saw the races but at least you were involved in the atmosphere.

In my teens, I became a member of the Hexham Male Voice Choir. One of the members took me along to one of the practices, which was held in the Unionist club to see if I would enjoy being in the choir. At that time the choir had about fifty members and I found them all very friendly. I really enjoyed my time as a member. I was in the choir until I left to go into the forces.

Over the years we would hold our practices in various places, the ones I remember being the Unionist club, West End Chapel and there was a church on Hencoates, which was also one of our venues. In fact, I visited one of the members a short time ago and although getting on in years, he still plays an active part in the choir.

He had a photograph of the choir on his wall, taken in the church on Hencoates. I was in it, so it brought back happy memories. He was one of three brothers in the choir; in fact, it was his youngest brother who took me to join the choir in the first place. The main venue during my time was my old junior school on the Sele where we would practice every Thursday night. During the winter months we would give concerts around the area. After the concert, the organisers would always lay on a good tea.

However, the highlight of the year was the competition we entered, which was held in Blackpool at the end of October. The choir would hire buses, and we would be off to Blackpool for the weekend. There were always big entries for the competitions but we used to do quite well.

Figure 6. Hexham Male Voice Choir, c. 1952. Author seventh from the left in front row.

One of the other choirs to enter in Blackpool – although I think they were a bigger choir than us and therefore in a different category – was the Prudhoe Gleemen. Just recently my sister-in law sent me a video of them performing in their centenary year, so it was nice to hear them and to know that they were still going strong after all these years.

After I left school the first football team I played for was Acomb Juniors. At this time Acomb was a mining village about three miles from Hexham. I played with the juniors for a while and then had a spell with the first team. Later I had a couple of seasons with Bardon Mill, who played in the Hexham and District league. The year that I was to join the army I started the season with Hexham-Shire but I only played a few games for them before I was called up. We would play the games on the Saturday afternoons, and on the Sunday the locals would get together on the Sele, pick a couple of teams, and play all afternoon.

We didn't bother with how many were in the side or having a referee, we just got on with the game and thoroughly enjoyed it. After the game we would go down to the burn at Cockshaw. Alongside the burn there was a path, and beside the path there was a small well with water running all the time. Whether it was the exertion of playing football or what, I don't know, but the water was beautiful.

One comment I must make is about the ball. We played with a leather ball which was quite heavy, even more so if it was wet. If you headed the ball and didn't get it just right, you would know about it. If the goal-keeper could clear the ball to the halfway line he was doing well. Today you see the players just stroke the ball and it carries a great distance, and as for the goal-keepers they can kick the length of the pitch no problem.

I did get a couple of games for the Hexham and District league select team; these games were played on Hexham Hearts ground. I can't remember what league Hexham Hearts were in but they had quite a good team at that time. My mates would play for different teams so we would meet up on a Saturday in the snooker club at the bottom of Priestpopple and catch up on the day's events before heading off for the night.

At that time the cattle mart was near the centre of the town, they quite recently moved to make way for the new hospital. The place they moved is where Hexham Hearts had their ground just beside Tyne Green.

Earlier with my job, I had been transferred to the Road Motor Engineers Department, to the Greenfield Works in Gateshead, which meant catching an early morning train to start at seven-thirty. I wouldn't be home until after six o'clock at night so it was a long day, the working week at that time being forty-five hours.

Although when I had started the job I had been working for the L.N.E.R. I was now working for British Rail. In the days of the L.N.E.R., the country was split into different areas run by different

Figure 7. Junior football at Tyne Mills, Hexham. Keith Irving played Left-half position. 5 May 1951.

companies. I hadn't been working very long when they were nationalised and became British Rail. At this time, I had a girlfriend (now my wife) and she came from Inverness, so I spent a couple of holidays up in the Highlands of Scotland.

In those years, the journey from Hexham to Inverness would take forever. You would leave Hexham early in the morning, get to Newcastle and catch a train for Edinburgh. From there you would get a connection for Inverness, arriving in Inverness after eight o'clock at night. I found Inverness a very pleasant town with a population of about thirty thousand. My girlfriend's family had a croft overlooking Loch Ness so it was a happy holiday away from it all.

One of the reasons I decided to look back was to try and give you a picture of the way of life during the thirties and forties.

There is no doubt, not my mind anyway, that we came from a far more disciplined background than the youngsters of today. In my opinion a large part of the reason for this was the fact that in the vast majority of cases your mother was always at home. She was the boss and you respected her for it. Although, at times, we would try and rebel, not always wanting to do what we were told. At the end of the day, you knew you would have to do it so it was best to get on with it. In a sense, although you didn't know it, you were prepared for army life; you were used to being told what to do and getting on with it, not a lot different from the army, really. Do what you were told, keep your head down, and get on with it.

Can you imagine the youngsters of today accepting orders without question? Somehow, I can't – but having said that, although I think that the officers and N.C.O.s would have a tough time bringing them into line, I think given time they would get the message across and the youngsters would probably start to enjoy it.

However, whether national service is the answer to society's problems is highly debatable. It would be a huge step to take. I personally think not, what the answer is I don't know. Successive governments have tried, but so far haven't managed to come up with a solution.

CHAPTER SIX

So, it's back to the run up to me joining the army. I've called the book 'The Reluctant Soldier' and I think it aptly describes how I – and I'm sure millions of others – felt at being called away from family and home for two years. But that was just it – the vast majority of men at that age were all in the same boat.

A while before my call up, I had been suffering from a terrible toothache so I went to see the dentist. He extracted the tooth that was causing the problem, and afterwards as we were chatting I told him I would be joining the army very shortly. He suggested he should put my teeth in good order before I went in. I thought this was a good idea, so that's what he did. It turned out very well as I didn't have any problems during my army time.

About a week before I was due to go in, I developed this awful cough; now, I wasn't normally prone to coughs and colds but this one was really bothering me. So much so that I decided I would go and see the doctor. I've got to admit hoping he would say I wasn't fit to report for duty, but as I was living in cloud cuckoo land, he didn't.

A few months before I was due to leave, my girlfriend and I decided to become engaged, so the nearer the time came for me to leave the more difficult it became to accept that I would be away for two years.

Having said that, I met a friend of mine the other day, who had served during the Second World War. He was looking very smart and proudly wearing his badge on his blazer. Now, this was someone who had been in the army for six and a half years, serving in foreign lands, not knowing if they would ever see their loved ones again. Can you imagine being called up with no end in sight, and you were there until the job was done? I suppose it says a lot about the British character in those days that they would accept they had a duty to do and off they would go. So, looking at it that way, the fact that I was going for two years and I would get the occasional leave really put the whole thing into perspective.

Everything was going well. I knew the date it would end and I would be back in civvy street and able to get on with life. So, it was a case of doing the rounds, saying goodbye to my relations and friends. The most difficult part of all was saying goodbye to my fiancé but that was it, I had to go.

Because of the long distance between Hexham and Honiton, I would have to leave the day before. On the given day, I left Hexham and travelled down to Newcastle. At Central Station, I met up with a chap who was also heading for Honiton in Devon. We'd never met before but we must have had the same look about us because we got to chatting and found out that we were both heading for the same place. Funnily enough I didn't come across him at the R.E.M.E. camp, but we actually lived on the same estate years after we had left the army.

It was a long journey, so we travelled overnight and after a couple of changes we arrived in Honiton in the middle of the morning. There must have been fifty men getting off the train, none of us knowing what to expect, but we soon found out there were three N.C.O.s waiting for us.

We were all lined up in threes, something we would soon become very used to, and off we marched to the camp. As we marched along, a chap came towards us, who we'll call the village idiot for want of a better expression. He got alongside and called out, 'So you think that I'm stupid'. We had to laugh but there was no doubt that the laugh was on us.

In due course we arrived at the camp where we were booked in, told which platoon we were in, and given our accommodation, which turned out to be a wooden hut with about a dozen beds in it. We met the N.C.O.s who would be in charge of us for the next two weeks. After that we would be transferred to another company for four weeks and this would be for our training and square bashing. The day of arrival was all about getting the paperwork in order and bringing us up to date with what would be happening in the next few days.

The next morning it was up with the larks being shouted at to rise and shine – I'm sure it was four o'clock in the morning. Find your way to the washrooms, which consisted of a long trough with everyone jostling for position. Knowing that you hadn't time to mess about, you would have to go for breakfast and be back ready for parade.

You would assemble outside your hut and then be marched off to the Quartermaster's stores, where you would be issued with your uniform – I was going to say 'fitted', but I think that would be stretching the point. The staff were pretty good though, they would take one look at you and hand you a uniform and they were never far off the mark. Although I'm pretty sure you were checked out and if it wasn't right they would have it altered. I didn't particularly like the uniform but it was passable. However, the greatcoat was just something else, what a weight was in it, if you had to wear it for any length of time you'd be exhausted. I must admit that I was never happy with my greatcoat; it just fitted where it touched.

Then you would be issued with your boots, kit bag, and all the other gear you would need. Once you had all that it was safe to say you were beginning to look like a soldier. There was a good mix of chaps in the hut, everyone prepared to make the most of it, so we soon got to know each other.

After you'd got all that sorted out, it was time to go for the *infamous* haircut. You'd often heard about the army haircuts, so it was with some trepidation that you went along to the barber's shop. I've got to say that you weren't disappointed. All the tales you'd heard had been no exaggeration. The barber would ask you how you would like your haircut, and of course you being totally green in the ways of the army would say, 'Just tidy it up, please'. At which point the barber would say, 'All you get here son is short back and sides and there won't be much left on the top either'. So, on that day there was a lot of young men's pride and joy left on the barber's shop floor. What made it even worse, you had to pay for it.

So, it was; always being pushed around, told to be here, there and everywhere during the day, never a minute to spare. After the efforts of the day there was still no time for relaxation. As soon as you got back from dinner your thoughts turned to your kit. Although one of the first jobs was to parcel up your civilian clothes. They had to be sent home as you weren't allowed to wear civilian clothes at the training camp. Everything had to be ready for the next day, pressing your uniform so you became a dab hand with the iron, blancoing your belt and gaiters.

Also, all the rest of your kit had to be brought up to scratch, one of the most important things – although everything had to be just right – was your boots. You were issued with two pairs of boots, one for working and one for best. The ones for best had been, what they called 'bulled up', which meant working on them until they had a perfect shine. The toes would have wee dimples on them which you would iron out, then we would apply the polish and keep rubbing it in for hours. It was a never-ending job, but luckily it got easier as time went on.

When my father had been in the army, he had to polish all his buttons, which I'm sure was a tedious job, but luckily by the time I was in they had done away with them and were using stay-bright buttons. So, it was one less job to do. You had to be thankful for small mercies.

Another thing you had to do in the morning before parade was to make up a bed block. This meant that you had to fold your blankets and sheets in a certain way and form them into a block. This block had to be a certain size and set up at the head of your bed. The N.C.O.s would measure it to make sure you had set it up correctly. There were inspections every morning; either the officer or the sergeant would walk round examining everyone's kit. Everything had to be just right or you were made to do it all over again. Believe me, they were very fussy, with very few – or indeed any – getting it right the first time.

There was a big cook house on the camp and you'd have to wait in long queues for your meals. However, the food was reasonably good with all the running about that you were doing. You were always looking forward to the next meal. Not that it was anything like your mother's home cooking but at least you could eat it.

In the second week I had to go to another camp for trade tests. This was to see where they would place you after your training was finished. I'm not sure where this camp was but the name Blandford seems to stick in my mind.

Anyway, one thing I do remember is that the food was awful. The first time I went into the cook house I saw plates laden with food and thought, 'This is great'. But I'm afraid most of it went into the bin.

They had a sergeant cook who would be dishing out the potatoes; he had them in a small bath, and a long-handled ladle. He would take the ladle full of potatoes and bang it down onto the edge of the bath, the potatoes would flop onto your plate. That is unless you were new to the system and held your plate up too high. The result of this being that he hit your plate and smashed it. Needless to say, you soon learned to keep your plate at a safe distance, or, if you were lucky, you would see it happening to someone else so you were forewarned.

Before I started the tests, I was called into this big room and told to sit at one end. An officer came in and sat at a desk at the other end of the room. He would question you very closely about what you had been doing prior to joining the army and what you'd had experience with during your apprenticeship. I must say that in those days all the officers came from the upper classes and they all spoke with a posh accent or no accent at all.

That's how they were perceived by me anyway, and I don't think I was far wrong. Not like today, where your accent doesn't play any part in your ability to carry out your duties and the way you are perceived. I'm writing about seventy years ago, so things have certainly changed in that time in more ways than one. The officer then told me that I would have to go through a series of tests to see if I needed any further training associated with being a mechanic.

So off I went to prepare for the various tests that had been set up for me. Over the next two days I sat the tests. I enjoyed it, as it was a pleasant change to be away from your own camp and doing something more along the lines that you were used to. The results of the tests you would receive at a later date, so then it was off back to Honiton and once again back into the full swing of army life.

One of the first things you were given when you arrived in Honiton was your army number. This was an eight-digit number unique to you and would be used all through your army service. It was stressed how important it was to get to know this number by heart as soon as possible. When you were reporting anywhere you would have to spring to attention. If it was an officer, you would have to salute, say your number, rank, and name, followed by, 'Reporting for duty, sir'. Even though it's a long number I can still remember it to this day.

Apart from me, there were other tradesmen, but a large number were eighteen-year-olds, who had never been away from home. Most of them would settle down quickly, but there were a few, who found it very difficult to settle and they would really miss home. But given time they would realise it was a whole lot easier to make the best of it and get on with it.

Another thing that was happening at that time was the injections that we had to have. I'm not sure what they were all for but I'm sure there would be a good reason behind them. One in particular, we were all lined up on the road side – probably about two hundred men – to have an injection. It was a case of rolling up your sleeve and waiting for the medical officer to reach you. He would be followed by a medical orderly with a tray of syringes. I don't remember the syringes being changed very often, either. I'm sure the one syringe would be used for a few injections. A number of the men would collapse in a heap at the sight of the medical officer approaching them. I don't think this would get them off the hook; they were just delaying the inevitable.

Another injection was one that I didn't like at all, although I've got to admit I wasn't very fond of any of them. For this one, the medical officer was sitting at a table, you had to put your arms on the table with your forearms facing up, and have an injection in each arm. What it was for, I've no idea. One of the injections must have had quite severe side effects as we were given twenty-four hours off. However, one platoon, although I don't think they were ordered to do anything, took it upon themselves to do a bit of gardening. This didn't prove to be a good idea as a few of them finished up in the medical centre.

During the first two weeks, when we were returning to the billet after dinner, we would meet these chaps running to the cook house. They were always running to catch the cook house open at the last minute. They knew that we were part of the new intake and that we would be following them into their company.

They would give us a shout as they passed, they never had the time to stop, 'We hope that you don't get the sergeant that we have, he's a holy terror we're always on the go'. They were in the company that we would be transferred to at the end of our two weeks. Needless to say, you wouldn't need three guesses to know who's platoon I finished up in.

CHAPTER SEVEN

After two weeks we were transferred to our new company and to our new platoon, where we would be training and square bashing for the next four weeks. And of course, to meet our new sergeant. I'm sorry to say this, but the men, who used to tell us about him, hadn't exaggerated one little bit.

This was a man who would show no mercy, we were straight into the routine from day one. It was a hard time, all the exercise made you very fit and, although I've said before the food wasn't brilliant, it was adequate, and you were always ready for the next meal.

At no time did you feel in charge of your own destiny, everything was done to order with the whole day being accounted for. You'd be back in the billet after dinner to get all your gear ready for the next day. But still, you were all in it together, the crack (conversation) was good, they were a happy bunch and we would help each other out. The billet was the usual wooden hut, though the weather was quite good so we were comfortable enough.

There was one parade that I looked forward to with at least a little bit of pleasure. This was the pay parade, everyone was assembled into a big hanger so there would probably be about two hundred on parade. You were called out in alphabetical order, so depending on your surname initial, you could be standing there for hours. One thing about this parade was that you would be standing easy, which made a whole lot of difference. Luckily, I wasn't too far down the list so my wait wasn't too long.

Upon hearing your name being called, you would spring to attention and march up to the desk, stand at attention, salute, and give your rank, name, and number to the officer in charge of the parade. You would be given your money, sign for it, salute again, about-turn, and then you could march back to your billet. You didn't get very much, so it was a long wait for very little.

A few months afterwards, I was on pay parade, this time charged by a very young officer. The officer flicked every note between his thumb and forefinger, doing this all afternoon. The pay corporal was telling me afterwards that he had a huge blister between his thumb and forefinger. No doubt he was making doubly sure he didn't make any mistakes.

The training we were put through at this time was relentless and sometimes even ruthless. On one occasion, we were ordered to get our full kit and be out on parade, and given very little time to get it together. Once on parade the sergeant gave us a quick inspection, then it was off at the double on a long march. After a while we came to this long steep hill. By this time everyone was flagging – one poor lad in particular feeling the pace very badly – so the sergeant ordered the chap behind to push him to the top. You can imagine that was one day we were pleased to get back to the billet.

Every day one of the platoon would be ordered to be the billet orderly for the day; this meant the orderly would have to stay in the billet and be responsible for everything in it. The inspections were always very tough and you wouldn't think it would be possible for them to get any worse.

But that's an understatement, when it was announced that the colonel would be coming around on a certain day to inspect the barrack rooms. It really did get worse with the N.C.O.s making doubly sure nothing would be left to chance on the day, especially with the sergeant who made it very plain that if the colonel found anything to complain about, he would take it personally and it wouldn't be hard to guess who would pay for it. So, you can imagine I wasn't too pleased to find out that on the day of the inspection it was my turn to be the billet orderly.

One redeeming feature was that there was a strong rumour going around the camp. On one of these inspections, supposedly the colonel had asked the orderly where he came from. Then he told the adjutant to give the orderly a weekend pass. This changed the whole complexion of the inspection for me – I was really up for it and looking forward to it. In due course the colonel arrived, followed by the adjutant, and I was sure the sergeant major would be tagging along, as well as another N.C.O. taking notes.

I sprang to attention saying my number, rank, name, and, 'Room ready for inspection, sir'. After walking around taking a good look at everything, he turned to me and asked me where I came from. This is it, I thought, getting ready for the weekend pass. But I'm afraid to say there was no mention of it much to my disgust. However, he seemed pleased with the way that the room had been presented so we had to be thankful for that. No doubt the N.C.O.s were relieved too – it wouldn't have gone down well if the room hadn't come up to scratch.

Another day we were ordered to turn out on parade with our full kit; we started marching up and down, as soldiers do. When it started to rain very heavily, it got so bad that the sergeant decided to head back to the billet. As we got to the billet one of the men said something that annoyed the sergeant – which, believe me, wasn't very difficult – as he wasn't noted for his sense of humour. He ordered the chap to run around the outskirts of the camp many times. The sergeant carried on giving us a lecture about something or other.

After a while the chap returned and because of the heavy rain he had his waterproof cape over his kit. It had been a warm humid day so steam was rising off him. The sergeant looked him up and down and asked him where he had been.

'Running around the camp so many times as ordered, Sergeant,' he answered.

'Oh, is that right?' said the sergeant, 'So, what took you so long, go and do it all again and make it quicker this time.'

Another day we were ordered to get all our kit together and out on parade in double quick time. After the inspection to make sure we all had our kit on correctly, he started to march us up and down for what, to us, seemed hours. It got to the stage where sergeants from other platoons were coming across and telling him that we'd done enough. Yet, I'm afraid it was like water off a duck's back, he wouldn't stop until he was ready. It certainly toughened you up, but you weren't finished for the day. Being out and about with all your kit meant that you would have to get it back up to scratch ready for inspection the next morning. There was no rest for the wicked, or the weary.

Every few days you would be given a duty which involved doing jobs around the camp. Everyone would have to take a turn, so it was pretty much a lottery what jobs you would finish up with. One of my duties was going along to the cook house and doing the spuds. There was a machine for doing the rough work but they had to be finished by hand. There were mountains of them so you were well and truly sick of the sight of potatoes by the time you were finished.

Another one I had to do was in the N.A.A.F.I. This was where you could go in the evenings for a cup of tea and a cake if you could manage to get time off. This was a cushy job just keeping the place tidy, clearing tables or whatever needed to be done. This was more my style, plenty of people about, being able to chat with other men and compare notes. It was always good for a laugh.

One of my other jobs was keeping the toilet block clean and tidy for a day; not a job I relished, but it had to be done. All these jobs had to be done after the training was finished for the day. This didn't mean you were excused having your kit ready for the next day, that still had to be done.

One thing I forgot to mention – and this was really a must – was that every day, usually after dinner, you would have to go and read company orders. If you didn't, and your name happened to be on it for some reason or other, then you could be in serious trouble for failing to report somewhere. Excuses for not turning up would not be accepted, you would just have to accept the consequences of your actions.

Usually this meant being put on a charge and appearing before the Company Commander. Inevitably this resulted in a few days' jankers, and then at the end of the day you would have to report to the guard house and be given even more jobs about the camp.

Every morning after breakfast, and having finished the chores around the billet, we would have to go on to the parade ground. First the sergeant would inspect everyone before the officer arrived on the scene. The sergeant would walk along the lines looking everyone up and down, ordering you to do this, that or the other, if he considered that you didn't come up to standard. So, you got used to being shouted at, and being told what he expected of you the next day.

One morning he came along, stopped at me, looked me up and down as usual and then said, 'Get a haircut.' It didn't make any difference if you needed one or not, that's what you were ordered to do. So, at the first chance I got, I was off to the barber shop.

The next morning I'm on parade sporting my new haircut. The sergeant walks along the lines, gets to me, and says, 'Get a haircut.' I know you were supposed to take everything thrown at you without question, but this was a bit much.

So, I said, 'I had a haircut yesterday, Sergeant.'

To which, he barked, 'Get another one today.'

I'm sure the sergeant and the barber were in cahoots, as when you were leaving the barber shop he would say, 'Tell the sergeant to send more men along', so maybe the sergeant was on commission. However, it completely slipped my mind, I forgot to tell the sergeant. The barber was a civilian, who must have been making a good living as he was cutting hair nonstop all day. I cannot remember if I went for the second haircut or not but I probably did – anything to keep the peace.

The first few days on the parade ground we were absolutely hopeless. Trying to march in an orderly fashion was totally beyond us. One thing we all perfected in double quick time was the soft shoe shuffle, as we desperately tried to get back into step.

I know this was new to all of us and it would take time for us to get working together. But in my opinion one of the main reasons why we were so slow, was the fact that all the N.C.O.s had a different style of shouting the orders. Some shouted, some barked, and some yelled whilst others simply just screamed – with the result that it took some time to pick up the order they were giving you. Also, it wasn't easy for about thirty men to pick up what they were saying and act upon it at the same time.

So, in the beginning it wasn't unusual to have one half of the platoon marching in one direction and the other half marching in the opposite direction. If the platoon was marching away from the sergeant and he shouted, 'SQUAD ABOUT TURN', the back of the squad would about turn while the front would keep on marching. At that, the sergeant would have a few choice words to say to the platoon.

I think they must have all come from the same school, as their language would be very colourful and they most certainly didn't mince their words. There were always a few platoons practicing on the parade ground at the same time. They would find it very amusing if it was us that got it all wrong. Just as we would find it very funny if it was them making the mistakes.

The thing was, as the days and weeks passed you would feel a big improvement taking place. Now the platoon was working together and you started to enjoy being smart and working together as a team. Of course, one of the big incentives to do well was the rivalry between the platoons – you always wanted to be ahead of the rest.

The weapons played a big part in our training, we had all been issued with rifles and these played a big part in the parades. The only problem with rifles was the amount of time you would have to spend cleaning them after use. So that you became very familiar with four by two, this is what you used to clean the barrel of the rifle. You would pull it through the barrel, time after time, until you were satisfied that the barrel was clean. Or should I say until you were sure it would pass the inevitable inspection that would take place afterwards.

One day we were getting tuition on machine guns; you had to be able to strip the gun down and then put it back together. If a fault developed you would have to be able to clear the fault and get the gun back ready for action. This particular day, one of the lads was told to strip the gun and get it back together ready for action. Which is what he did, fixing the magazine onto the top of the gun and bringing it up to the firing position. He got it into position looking very professional with a job well done when the magazine fell off. So, there was much hilarity amongst the rest of us – even the sergeant had to have a wee smile. Although that didn't stop him from giving the lad a right row telling him what he thought of him. I must admit that I quite enjoyed these sessions.

One stroke of luck we had was that the sergeant went on leave for a few days. Not that the new one was much better, but at least he was different. I don't think he was impressed with me, one day he stuck his face into mine and said, 'You don't like me, do you?'

I've already said I was always prepared to stand my corner, but by the same token I'm not stupid; to answer him truthfully would have been the height of stupidity, so I said, 'I don't know you, Sergeant,' and luckily, he walked off. He was a lot younger than our sergeant but you have to give credit where it's due, he was always immaculate. He was a different kettle of fish to our regular sergeant but at the end of day, they had to achieve the same results so their aims were the same.

While all this was going on, every night you would have to get your kit ready for the next day's parades. So, we all became dab hands with the iron, although it's not a thing I'm very familiar with these days.

Of course, there were always the billet and kit inspections to contend with on a regular basis. Not something we looked forward to but nevertheless they all took time to prepare for.

The first inspection with the new sergeant, he arrived in the billet with a long-handled brush, we were all wondering what he was going to do with it, we soon found out. On top of your locker would be your kit and haversacks – all neatly folded and to us looking immaculate – the only problem being that it wasn't us carrying out the inspections. He would look at your kit and if he didn't like what he saw, he would swipe the whole lot off the locker and onto the floor.

You would have to have it all done properly for the next day's inspection. He was a very hard man to please, so it was very few that didn't have to do their kit again. As you can imagine, he wasn't a very popular man. I suppose if you'd asked him, his reply would have been that he wasn't in the job to be popular. Needless to say, we never asked him, to question his decisions would have only made it worse for yourself.

The best way of dealing with it was to accept it and get on with it, hoping your next efforts would meet with his approval. We used to console ourselves with the fact that we were only there for a short time and it wasn't going to last forever.

On the camp there was a big gymnasium, which was very well equipped with a team of physical training instructors who were well up to the job. They could really put you through the mill so that at the end of each session you would be exhausted, but at the same time you'd enjoy it. There's nothing like good physical exercise to get yourself fit. Looking back, I'm sure I would have been fitter than at any other time in my life. I would really enjoy it when we would get outside and have some competitive long-distance races. Pounding around the square for a few laps really worked up an appetite. We would have regular sessions in the gym, so it was something we all looked forward to.

We were in the camp for a month before we would be given a day off and would be allowed to leave the camp. So, on the Saturday, we would get ourselves spruced up and present ourselves at the guardroom. There you would be given a thorough inspection; if you didn't come up to scratch, you weren't allowed out, and believe me, if you thought that your sergeant was bad, the provost sergeant could be a whole lot worse. You would heave a sigh of relief when you made it past the guardroom.

Of course, you would have to go through the whole procedure again on your return, before you would be allowed back in. If you came back worse for wear, you could finish up in the guardroom for the night and still suffer the consequences the next day.

Luckily that didn't happen to me, but you would heave an even bigger sigh of relief once you were past the guardroom and safely back into camp. However, it was nice to get out and have a look around the area. Not that I can remember anything about Honiton, other than that it was very pleasant and it certainly made a nice change from what we had experienced in the previous weeks.

Devon is a beautiful county and the weather had been generally good over my time there – it was lovely autumn weather. It would start off quite cool in the early morning but it would get nice and sunny as the day went on. Our first parade would be on the square, and from the square you could see for miles.

On a nice calm morning with the mist hanging over the hills in the distance you could relax. That is until the sergeant started bawling again – quick march, right turn, left turn, about turn, halt, come on keep up – to the ones doing the soft shoe shuffle to get back into step. When we first started this had been a regular occurrence but now over the weeks, we had improved so there was just the occasional slip.

The following weekend, we got the chance to spend the day away from the camp again, so a few of us took a trip up to Exeter. On the Sunday, we would get the chance to relax, although we would have to get our gear ready for the Monday. The days were flying past; no wonder, with never a minute to spare being on the go from morning until night.

A few days before the end of my time in Honiton, my sergeant said to me, 'One of the other sergeants wants to see you, so report to him at the post room.' By sheer coincidence, this sergeant came from my hometown. I didn't know him personally but I did know who he was. Before he'd joined the army, he'd worked with my father at the Hexham General Hospital. Because he wanted to see me in the post room, I assumed he'd spotted the post mark on a letter to me. So, he'd sent for me to see if I was who he thought I was. Having confirmed that he knew my father very well and asking how he was keeping, he started to ask me about the time that I'd spent in Honiton.

What could I say, I could hardly start running the camp down, but as it happened, I didn't want to anyway. Certainly, there had been some rough times, but on the whole, I didn't have any complaints. You had to take the rough with the smooth, as far as getting the rough end of the sergeant's tongue, everyone would get their fair share; he didn't have any favourites. Usually if there was any trouble you would all be in it together.

So, the sergeant said if there was anything that he could help me with just to let him know. I thanked him but as I was leaving the camp in the next few days, I didn't think that I would be taking up his offer.

However, this sergeant was very well liked by his platoon, so it was a pity that I hadn't got him as my sergeant in the first place. The four weeks of training and square bashing were fast coming to an end, and the day of the passing out parade was looming large. So that the last few days were even more hectic we prepared for the final parade at Honiton.

On the day of the parade, we were all dressed in our best uniforms, boots shining, everything looking perfection. The N.C.O.s made sure there was nothing out of place. It was a nice day with everyone lined up on the square, waiting to be inspected by the colonel. Then we would be marching up and down in unison, hardly believing that just four weeks ago, it would have been impossible to imagine what we had achieved. The parade went well, with everyone being pleased with the results. As the days had passed, even the sergeant's bark didn't seem as bad as it was when we'd first started. Either that, or we were just getting used to him, I certainly can't imagine that he was mellowing with age.

Looking back, it must have seemed a daunting task for the N.C.O.s to have to lick us into shape in just four weeks. So, they might have been hard at the start but they didn't have time to mess about. For them, it was a case of get on with it and don't let anything or anyone get in the way. Most times, they had achieved what they had set out to do, though you would get the occasional soldier, who for some reason or other would be put back for a month.

We had one with us but gradually he would start to conform and by the end of the month he'd got the message and passed out with the rest of us. After the six weeks, you would be posted to where the army had decided to send you.

If you'd been in a regiment, it was more than likely that you would have been recruited from the same area so there was a good chance you would spend your two years with the same personnel. With us, we would all be heading off in different directions; over the six weeks you had made some good friends but there was a strong possibility that you wouldn't see them again.

We could be attached to one of the regiments or maybe finish up in a R.E.M.E. workshop. So, there was some excitement wondering where you would be posted to; it was a bit of a lottery, but you would have to wait until the assignments came through. On the day after the passing out parade, we were all assembled in a big hall, waiting to be given the paperwork telling us where we had been posted to.

We had a long wait as the assignments were late in coming through, so somehow, we had to fill in the time until they arrived.

There was a piano in the hall, and it was amazing the talent that appeared – one man was an excellent pianist and there were plenty of singers ready and able to give us a song. We were all in good spirits and it turned out to be an enjoyable time. At the same time, we were all a bit apprehensive wondering where we would be off to the next day and what it would be like when we got there.

CHAPTER EIGHT

Finally, they arrived, so there was a hectic half hour comparing notes with your mates, finding out where they were all going. I was being posted to Ellesmere in Shropshire, a place I'd never heard of, and I would be heading there by train the next day. I would be travelling with another two chaps. I didn't know them, but it was nice to have company for the journey and we soon became friends.

I would be going to Ellesmere for a month to take some training in the electrical side of the job. At the end of the month, it would be the Xmas holidays and after the holidays I would be posted to my permanent assignment. We had a long journey to the new camp, and we got there to discover it had once been an army hospital. So, the billets were long wooden huts with about thirty men in each. It was set on the edge of the town, so it was just walking distance to the town centre. Along the way you would have to pass a lake, so it was a pleasant walk.

You soon discovered that the discipline in the camp was much the same as Honiton, but there was a much more relaxed atmosphere about the place. The food was reasonably good and there was plenty of it, so I'm afraid all the good work I'd done in Honiton was very soon put behind me and I put on a bit of weight. There was time set aside for physical training, but the square bashing was practically non-existent. Of course, an army camp isn't an army camp if it doesn't have a parade ground and Ellesmere was no exception. After breakfast, we would parade on the square for roll call and some marching, but that was about it. One test we had to go through was a five-mile hike in our army boots and over rough terrain, and it had to be completed in under an hour.

Running wasn't allowed, you would have to walk at the double. We started off in good style until we came to a river, there was a ford but the water was still over the top of our boots. We decided to plough through it, but there was a fallen tree right across the river so some of the wide boys decided to cross using the tree. Unfortunately, the tree was very wet and slippery so they got so far across and slipped, getting soaked in the process; at least it was only our feet that got wet.

We kept going, and arrived back in the camp in under an hour, so we'd been successful and felt very pleased with ourselves. After we'd finished, the officers came around to check everyone's feet; there were quite a few men with blisters so they had to have some treatment, luckily mine were alright. I know that five miles in an hour is not that fast but you certainly had to keep moving. I kind of suspect, but I'm not sure, that if you didn't manage it in the hour, you would have to do it again.

After the parade in the mornings, we would be off to attend lectures in the classrooms, a total change from the previous six weeks. At the end of the session, we would have to sit an exam, which I passed, so in no time the course was over and Xmas leave was drawing ever closer.

One of the good things about this camp was that you were allowed out at the weekends, and as there were some big towns in the area, we could spend a pleasant day away. The camp was much freer and easier than Honiton; life seemed to go at a much steadier pace and you felt more relaxed for it.

One of the chaps who I'd become friendly with was an excellent pianist, I don't think he'd ever had any lessons – just picked it up by ear – but he could certainly rattle a tune out of the piano. On the days away, if we went into a pub and it had a piano, after a few tunes the landlord would ask him to stay and play for a while, and the drinks would be on the house. Needless to say, it was a good move on the landlord's part as everyone in the pub would be enjoying a good sing-song and, of course, staying there and buying more drinks.

Anyway, the time that we were all looking forward to had arrived, so it was time to pack and head home for the Xmas leave.

CHAPTER NINE

Leading up to the time for me to join the army, my fiancé and I had decided that if it was possible we would get married during the Xmas holidays. So, one of the first things I would have to find out would be if I would be getting leave at that time. On making enquiries, everything seemed to be in order, so my fiancé was able to go ahead with the arrangements.

Having arranged a meeting with the minister, they both concluded that the most suitable day for all concerned would be Xmas day. I've got to admit I didn't know they held weddings on Xmas day. I suppose it's quite rare for a wedding on Xmas day and as I've never met anyone else who got married on that day, it's possibly *very* rare. Anyway, that is what they decided, so Xmas day it would be.

The position that I was in meant I couldn't take part in any of the arrangements, so all that was left for me to do was turn up. Which I duly did and we were married on Xmas Day 1954 in the Trinity Church, on Beaumont Street in Hexham.

At that time, my aunt and uncle were managing a pub in the marketplace in Hexham so that's where the reception was held. Some of my wife's relatives managed to come down from Inverness, so with all my relatives from Hexham and the Consett area being there, a good time was had by all.

We celebrated our golden wedding last Xmas (2004) and decided to make a long holiday of it. Our eldest son and his family decided to emigrate to New Zealand six years ago; we did go and visit them four years ago. But we decided for our fiftieth anniversary we would go and spend Xmas and New Year with them. We have two granddaughters out there growing up very fast and although we keep in touch, it's not the same as spending time with them. On Xmas day we had a barbeque and enjoyed the outdoor life, but it is strange to go into the shops hearing Xmas carols being played, especially as the sun is shining outside and it's the middle of summer.

The rest of the time we went touring around the South Island, hired a car and covered a large area before heading back to Wellington. A few days with the family, then it was off to Auckland to spend a few days in that area, then back home.

Auckland is a lovely city and it's not called the 'City of Sails' for nothing; I've never seen so many boats anchored in the same place. New Zealand is a lovely country, good roads with not a lot of traffic as there isn't a big population. The scenery is very varied and the people are really friendly, so we had a good time.

One thing we did find handy in New Zealand, and we used them quite a lot, was The Returned Service's Associations (R.S.A.) Clubs. Every reasonably-sized town would have one and some of them would do meals, which we found to be good. We found the locals very helpful. They would go out of their way to show you where the clubs were situated. Although as the years pass by their memberships are dwindling and I'm sure they'll have to find new ways of keeping them going.

On this trip we decided to fly a new route to us. We used Emirates from Glasgow, and found the airline to be very good, and we were very pleased with the service. But anyway, back to national service, the leave soon passed and once again you're in the position of having to say goodbye. It never gets any easier.

CHAPTER TEN

You know how you hear rumours over the years and take very little notice? One I'd heard was that if you had to get a train connection at Crewe you could be waiting long enough. It turned out on the way back to camp that I had to connect at Crewe, and I seem to remember having a long wait. Finally, I got back to camp to meet up with my mates and wait for the new assignments to come through.

Now the thing was that my circumstances had changed; I was now a married man so I would have to find out how my wife could claim the marriage allowance, to which we would be entitled. At the first opportunity, I went to see the pay clerk. It all seemed a bit complicated so I suggested I should leave it and get it sorted at my next camp. However, the pay clerk was very good and said to leave it with him, he would get it sorted and let me know when it had all been completed. True to his word, he got in touch to say that everything was in order which meant that I could leave Ellesmere and not have to worry about anything, which was a relief.

So, we were back in the same situation as we'd been at the end of our time in Honiton, waiting to find out where we would be posted and what wonders lay ahead. This posting would be on a more permanent basis, at least as permanent as a posting in the army would ever be – you would never know what would be around the corner.

After a few days, the postings arrived and were put up on the notice board. One of them was for a camp less than twenty miles from my hometown. This would have been ideal for me but sad to say it was allocated to someone else, so that was that.

Looking back, I suppose I was a bit upset that I hadn't got that posting, but on reflection I think the posting I did get gave me the chance to travel a bit and broaden my horizons. I would be attached to the Worcestershire Regiment, who at that time were based in the Bulford Barracks in Salisbury. I looked back on my time in Ellesmere as time well spent; I'd made good friends there, the town and the surrounding area were very nice, so I'd enjoyed my stay.

Once again it was a case of packing all your gear together, saying goodbye to your friends, and heading off into the unknown. They, in turn, were heading off in all different directions, but life is funny. Maybe sometime in the future our paths would cross again. I left Ellesmere and travelled down to Salisbury by train. It was a long journey so it was late in the afternoon before I arrived at the camp.

My first introduction to the camp was seeing men standing at the side of a hut peeping around the corner. They waved me to keep back out of the way saying, 'We're avoiding the R.S.M. (Regimental Sergeant Major).' Which, I found out later, to be a good idea, as it turned out he was not a man to tangle with. I'm sure a lot of people had found that over the years.

I reported to the guardroom that I'd arrived and during the conversation discovered that in a few weeks' time the regiment was being posted to Germany, so my stay in Salisbury would be very short. I was shown round to where I would be billeted for the time that I would be in the camp.

Once again, the billet was a wooden hut. There was a stove in the middle of the hut, and as you can imagine the beds nearest the stove were in big demand, especially as it was in the middle of winter. More often than not, the N.C.O.s would pull rank and claim the beds nearest the stove. However, if they were kept well stocked up it wasn't too bad; I would certainly come across worse.

I soon found out that the move to Germany was in the advanced stages, the advance party had been away for some time and two of the R.E.M.E. contingent was with them. On my arrival it brought the R.E.M.E. strength to seven. We would be embarking very shortly to Germany to a place called Iserlohn. As usual we would have carried on keeping our kit up to scratch as there were the usual inspections.

One of the N.C.O.s was a good sign writer, and for a small fee he put my surname onto my kit bag so that when it was folded up, it would sit on the top of my locker with my name plain for everyone to see. At last, I was in the situation of being able to carry out the job I'd been trained for. The workshops were just wooden huts but you soon found your way around and got on with the job.

I found time to have a look around the Salisbury area. With it being winter, it wasn't looking at its best, but at least you got a good idea what was in the area. Of course, a must see was the very famous Stonehenge, a very impressive sight and at that time you were able to walk round it with no restrictions. I believe a lot of changes have taken place, not all for the better, I'm sure. You soon got to know your way around the camp and the people you were involved with, everyone being very friendly and making you welcome.

One day we were out of the camp for a visit to Salisbury, standing at a bus stop, and we got talking to this chap. We were telling him that in the not too distant future we were being posted abroad. He asked us where we were off to, and telling him we were heading for Germany, he said 'Germany? That's not abroad!', so obviously he'd been to more exotic places. Also, while I was there we did some manoeuvres on Salisbury Plains, which stood us in good stead for when we went to Germany, as a large part of the year was spent on manoeuvres around the German countryside.

One good thing that emerged from our posting, was that we were given a seventy-two-hour pass, and would be able to go home for a long weekend. Something I hadn't been expecting, so it was a pleasant surprise. Having enjoyed the break and once again back in camp, it was all systems go and straight into the final preparations for our departure. Our kit bag and haversacks were fully loaded and we were ready for off.

CHAPTER ELEVEN

We all boarded a train to London, arriving at one of the main line stations, there we would pick up a train to Harwich. At Harwich there would be a boat waiting for us to take us overnight to the Hook of Holland. This big boat – well it looked big to me anyway – was lying alongside the quay. We were all herded on and put down into the bowels of the boat. The thing I remember the most was the heat, as there were a lot of men crowded into a small space.

Over the years, I've heard all the antidotes for avoiding sea-sickness but this was my first experience of being on a boat – a boat of any size at least. We were each given a bunk which was something I suppose, not that it made much difference to me. I soon discovered I was a hopeless sailor, something which remains true to this day. Although I've got to say in my defence, that I wasn't the only one, not by a long way. Some of the lads were saying to lie on your bunk and don't move, that's the best way to avoid sea-sickness. So once the boat set sail I took their advice and lay on the bunk, but after a short time, I'm saying to myself I'd better go and find a toilet and make it quick. Luckily, I found one and it was a case of staying there the entire voyage. If you did leave it there was no doubt someone else would have rushed into it and there would be no way you would have found another one. While rushing to the toilet, I bumped into someone who turned around and shouted at me to watch where I was going. I'm afraid I didn't have time to stop and argue with him. He would more than likely have been covered with something he didn't like. However, all things come to an end, though not before I thought that I was going to die. I was wishing that I would die, it truly is a horrible experience. It was an overnight journey and must have been one of the longest nights of my life. We finally arrived in the Hook of Holland in the early hours of the morning. We disembarked and had a long walk carrying all our gear to a big hanger, where there was a breakfast ready for us.

They had laid a good breakfast out for us but to say that I didn't fancy it would be putting it mildly. As a matter of fact, at that time I didn't think I would ever look at food again. But I have to say, I like my food and after a couple of hours I was nearly back to normal and looking forward to the next meal.

In one way I was lucky because I'm sure a lot of the men were worse off than me and would take a lot longer to get over it. We all headed to where there was a train waiting to take us across Holland and into Germany. We were lucky we were travelling during the day, as it gave us the chance to admire the Dutch countryside. It was very flat and fertile and with no hills to block your vision, you could see for miles. The towns and villages all looked very clean and tidy. The train was very fast and comfortable, what a difference to the journey on the boat, it was lovely to sit back and enjoy the journey.

Sitting on the train, I had time to reflect on what had happened to me in the last three months. I was thinking that having been away from home on just the odd occasion, here I was heading for Germany, having spent a large part of my time in the army moving around in England. I'd moved up and down the country spending time in places I'd never even heard of, so I certainly did get about. From that point of view my experience with the army had been varied indeed. The discipline I could take – it could get tough – but on the whole, if you did what you were told to do and got on with it, that's probably as much as they expected from you.

I'd never been in a foreign country before and here I was crossing Holland and heading for Germany, wondering what was in store for me during the next 21 months. It wouldn't be long before I would start to find out. Iserlohn was drawing ever closer.

CHAPTER TWELVE

We arrived in Iserlohn to be met off the train. It was dark so we didn't get a first impression of the town other than there was plenty of snow about.

We were trucked up to camp and once there, we were allocated our accommodation. Now from the very start, there was no comparison between these barracks and the ones that we had been used to in Britain. These were ex-German army barracks built of stone and all centrally heated. Also, another big advantage, there were only six men to a room, which made it much homelier. We were welcomed by the two R.E.M.E. men, who had come across with the advance party. One was the Lance Corporal and the other was a craftsman, which was the rank I now held.

So, you can well imagine, arriving in Germany in the middle of winter to a centrally heated barrack room was sheer bliss. In Britain in the mornings, you would have to go outside to the washroom and toilets. Here everything was on the same floor, the only thing not on that floor was the shower room. It was on the ground floor, but there was always plenty of hot water.

We were on the first floor, with the Quartermaster's store on the ground floor and the band were on the top floor.

So, here I was in Germany, attached to The First Battalion of the Worcestershire Regiment and I would be in the M.T. Section. The camp was well set out and covered a big area. Obviously, the Germans had paid a lot of attention to their forces over the years. Their camps were permanent and well equipped compared to ours, which seemed to me to be wooden huts scattered here and there.

MYSELF AND THREE OTHER R.E.M.E.

PERSONNEL OUTSIDE THE WORKSHOP.

Figure 8. Keith Irving (right) with three other R.E.M.E. personnel outside the workshop.

INSIDE OF WORKSHOP.

Figure 9. Inside the workshop.

Once we had got ourselves settled in, we went off to explore the camp, to find the main building, which of course was the cook house. Then it was off to see the workshop and what the working conditions would be like over the coming months.

We needn't have worried, we had a good-sized workshop and they hadn't forgotten the central heating, so we had nothing to complain about. There were seven R.E.M.E. personnel attached to the Worcestershire Regiment, one sergeant, one lance corporal, and five craftsmen.

The sergeant and the lance corporal were both regulars, who would have signed on for a number of years. At that time the government, in their wisdom, was allowing men to sign on for three years. So, two of the craftsmen had signed on for the three years, the other three craftsmen and that included me were doing their national service. The lance corporal and the craftsman, who had come across in the advance party, had obviously been in the camp for a while. They showed us around so that we soon became familiar with the camp.

CHAPTER THIRTEEN

We had arrived in Iserlohn in the middle of winter, and it was very cold with deep snow on the ground. In the centre of the camp was a big square – the parade ground – which of course, you would think would be out of action, covered in deep snow. But I'm afraid that the regimental sergeant major had other ideas; it wasn't long before he had a squad of men armed with shovels clearing the snow, so that he could make a start with his beloved square bashing. The next day, we would see the men marching up and down enjoying the fruits of their labour (I don't think). The regimental sergeant major was the top ranking N.C.O. in the battalion and was a law unto himself – if he said jump you jumped, no questions asked.

I remember him as a man with a big handlebar moustache and big teeth. When he showed his teeth, he wasn't grinning at you, it was just a big snarl he had developed to perfection over the years. So, as I've said before, it was advisable to keep out of his way as much as possible.

He had a nickname, but I think I'd better keep it to myself, in case he ever has the privilege of reading this. In any case, there would be no doubt he would know what it was, although I'm positive no one would have the audacity to say it to his face.

He would be the colonel's right-hand man, as the men were concerned, if you saw the colonel about the camp the R.S.M. wouldn't be far behind. We would have very little contact with him other than seeing him about the camp.

But one day an orderly arrived at the workshop to tell the sergeant he had to send one of the craftsmen to the R.S.M.'s office to report to the R.S.M. The sergeant was hoping he would get a volunteer, which was wishful thinking on his part. The thing was we were dressed in denims and as we were working around trucks all the time, we weren't the smartest soldiers on the block. So, our theory was that if we went anywhere near the R.S.M., there was a good chance we would finish up on a charge. In the end, the sergeant decided he was fighting a losing battle and said to me, 'You go and see what the R.S.M. wants.'

It was with some trepidation that I went along, found him in his office and reported to him. He would have to be called 'sir'; the only difference between reporting to him and reporting to an officer, was that you didn't have to salute.

The thing was, he was always smartly dressed and it was quite easy to mistake him for an officer, especially if you were new to the camp. So, on seeing the R.S.M. approaching, they would decide not to take a chance and salute him anyway. At this, he would growl at them, 'You don't salute me, boy!', but maybe secretly he was quite pleased as his bark didn't seem to be quite so bad.

Anyway, I reported to him, he looked me up and down and I thought, *That's it, I'm going to be charged.*

But he said, 'What do you want?'

So, I said, 'You've sent for a craftsman, sir.'

He replied, 'Oh yes, I've got a job that I want doing.'

It turned out he'd had a sign made and he wanted it fitted on the wall outside his office. I went back to the workshop, got some tools, and went back and fitted it. He seemed pleased with the result, so I was off heaving a big sigh of relief.

Really speaking, apart from the fact that you still had to keep your kit up to scratch – with there always being the inevitable inspections and, of course, keeping your room tidy – it was pretty much like having a job in civvy street. You would be up in the morning, have a wash and a shave, make up your bed block, tidy the room and be off to breakfast. After that you would go down to the workshop to start work at 8 o'clock. With a break for meals you would be working all day finishing at 5 o'clock.

Although, if we were very busy with a lot of work, we would have to go back after dinner for two or three hours. One of the perks with this, was that the sergeant made arrangements with the duty cook that we would get supper. The duty cook would rustle up something for us, which was usually very good. The food at the camp was passable – once again not home cooking, but you survived.

We were always kept busy, as there was a lot of transport with an infantry battalion and a big variety of equipment. Really you were increasing your knowledge, not just filling in time. I suppose that made the time pass quicker, but still not quick enough. Our time was spent on maintenance and repairs, which kept us on the go.

We had a store where we kept the essentials, but it didn't stock a big range of spares, so any job that was considered to be to big would be sent to a R.E.M.E. workshop, which was a good thing. We would leave in the morning to go a distance away to the workshop and not be back until late afternoon, it filled the day in nicely. These workshops were spacious with good working conditions and the most up to date equipment. There were German mechanics working alongside the R.E.M.E. personnel.

Occasionally I would go to the workshops to sit trade tests, as the army liked to keep up to date and increase your skills. When you passed these tests, you were given extra stars, so I accumulated quite a few and I seem to think you got extra pay when you passed.

I mentioned Germans working in the R.E.M.E. workshops; there were married quarters attached to the regiment. So, there were school kids, who had to be taken to school by bus. There were a few Germans working about the camp, the ones I would come into contact with were the drivers of the school buses. If there were any problems with the buses, they would come into the workshop to have them sorted. They also would wash their buses in the wash bay attached to the workshop, so you got to know them quite well. I found them very pleasant and easy to get on with, though I did see one or two of them get a bit upset if the subject of politics was brought up. As long as you kept away from politics, you would get on fine.

There had been a lot of damage in Germany during the war, signs of which were – in some places – plain to see. One thing I did notice at that time was that the German people were very hard working. You would see them starting work early in the morning and they would be still hard at it late at night. I suppose at that time there would be a lot of work to be done so they were certainly getting on with it.

CHAPTER FOURTEEN

On our arrival in Iserlohn, one of the first things we discovered was that cigarettes were very cheap. I think they were subsidised; each person being allowed to buy so many at a shilling a packet (five new pence). As you can imagine, the number of chain-smokers shot up overnight.

I've got to say, it didn't affect me as I wasn't a smoker and didn't see the reason to start because they were cheap. I've never smoked a cigarette in my life, however the fact that they were so cheap was just a novelty to most people and once the novelty had worn off, they soon returned to smoking their normal quota. They were handy in one way; if anyone back home was a smoker, when you went on leave you could always take them a few hundred fags and they would be very much appreciated. You could buy all the popular brands, so it wasn't cheap rubbish they were trying to get rid of, and they most certainly didn't have all the health warning signs on the packets that they do today.

As I've already said, we were billeted on the first floor of a three-storey block. The band were on the floor above. So, we could often hear them practising; they were very good and very professional. I'm sure a lot of musicians in those days would get their skills from the time they'd spent in the forces. We would see them practising outside, marching up and down preparing to travel to other regiments when they would be having their parades. On occasion, they would give a concert in the N.A.A.F.I. (Navy, Army and Air Force Institutes). They could play all types of music. The concerts would draw a big crowd and be thoroughly enjoyed by everyone.

This is the second time I've mentioned the N.A.A.F.I. and it's just dawned on me that I'm not a hundred percent sure what it stands for. I looked it up in the dictionary, it stands for Navy, Army, Air Force Institute.

It was a cafe based in the camp, where you could go for your morning break, have a cup of tea and a biscuit. In the evening, you could go there for a meal if you could afford it. We would sometimes do this at the weekends, it being a nice change from the cook house.

CHAPTER FIFTEEN

The M.T. Section was part of the Headquarter Company. All the drivers in the battalion were in it, so there were quite a large number of men in the section, as you'll see on the photograph on the next page. I look at the photo and although I recognise faces, for the life of me, I cannot remember their names. I'm sure I'll be forgiven as it was a long time but we all got on well together and they were good to work with.

Once I'd left I didn't see any of them again. That's not strictly true; years later, I'd moved to Inverness and was living on my wife's family croft. I was driving through the town one day and I spotted the M.T.O. (Motor Transport Officer) and another chap walking along the street. He was the Captain in charge of the M.T. Section when I was with the Worcesters.

I didn't get the chance to stop and speak to him, but there was a Round Britain Powerboat Race taking place at the time with a lot of powerboats anchored in the harbour. I've assumed to this day that he would be taking part in it; he was always into big cars and motorbikes, so powerboats could have easily appealed to him. Anyway, that's him in the centre of the photograph.

Figure 10. The Worcestershire Regiment, M.T. Section. The First Battalion. 1955

As it got towards Easter, the battalion started to prepare to go into the German countryside on exercises. This involved part of the battalion being away from the camp for two or three weeks at a time, taking part in manoeuvres with other regiments in the area. Sometimes we would be sleeping outside, sometimes in tents, but generally roughing it. We would get our gear together and head into the wide unknown, not knowing what to expect, but having to cope with anything that was thrown at us. So, from the end of April until October 1955, I would spend a lot of my time away from the camp, returning for a short while, and then off again.

It could be quite enjoyable but a lot depended on the weather, although I did find that the summers in Germany were generally quite good. The winters were a lot colder than at home, although it was cold and dry, while at home it wouldn't be as cold but it would feel very damp. On my first time away, we were camping under some huge trees with plenty of leaves on them to give us shelter. We had all the waterproof gear, so we were confident that we had all eventualities covered. That is until it started to pour down. When the rain drops got passed, the leaves started to hit your waterproofs and the noise they made certainly put you off sleeping. After that, I vowed I would think more carefully about where I would sleep.

On these exercises, there would be other regiments involved, pitting their wits against each other, so you would always be on the lookout for enemy activity. One night we were on standby, keeping a watchful eye for any activity in the area, and after a couple of hours we were stood down.

Some bright spark must have decided that a cup of tea wouldn't go amiss, so the ration truck was sent round with tea. Although the thought was well meant, I think they must have forgotten for how long the tea had been made. It was absolutely stewed and I remember it lying on my stomach like a brick all night; I suppose I was a fool for drinking it, but you live and learn.

It was our job as R.E.M.E. mechanics to keep the vehicles moving, so we would always be at the rear of the convoy. If there were any problems you would have to make a quick assessment and if possible sort it out on the spot. If it was going to take some time you would tow it to the next stop and, hopefully, get the time to sort it and get it back on the road.

One day I was sent to look at a vehicle with engine problems. It appeared at that time, we would be staying in the area for some time. I decided I would start stripping the cylinder head as the gasket was blown. I was well into the job when an officer comes and says, 'Get packed up, we're moving out.'

It was bad enough having to work in those conditions, without having to get things together and moving on, but that was it, that's what you had to do. So, it was a case of hunting around for someone to give you a tow and hoping you would get the time to finish the job at the next stop. One good thing that we had in our favour was that we had a team of dispatch riders, whose job it was to keep the convoy together. They would look for any problems ahead, and of course, if we had problems at the back they would keep in touch so we would know where to go, after we'd gotten the problem sorted. They were experts at whizzing in and out of the traffic so we relied on them a lot.

There were a few different areas where we carried out these exercises, the Sennelager Plains being one where we spent a lot of time; this was a huge area, ideal for carrying out the exercises. We would spend time in the area, then we would head back to camp for a while, and then we would be off again on another expedition into the great unknown.

I must admit I quite liked these exercises. You were always on the move with plenty to occupy your mind so the time seemed to go far quicker than when you were in camp. Although, when you did get back to camp there was always a lot to do getting the vehicles ready for the next exercises.

CHAPTER SIXTEEN

About this time, all the craftsmen were in the camp together when we were all summoned to the M.T.O.'s office. This sounded very ominous; we would be in and out of the office all the time, but for the five of us to have to appear in front of him together made us think something out of the ordinary was going on. So, we all assembled in his office to be told he'd received orders he had to transfer two of us to another camp.

The five of us all had about the same service and still some considerable time to go. The reason for the postings was that another unit had been posted to either Singapore or Hong Kong (I'm not sure which). Two of their craftsmen only had a few months to go so that was the reason why two of us were being transferred.

I can still visualise us, standing there and thinking to myself that I was quite happy where I was and could do without the hassle of moving on.

The M.T.O. had decided he would accept volunteers. In the event of him not getting two volunteers, he would have to decide who would have to go, and his decision would be final. There was a long silence then much to my relief anyway, he got his two volunteers. One of the three-year men and one of the national servicemen decided they would like to give it a go. So, the M.T.O. was happy and I think the rest of us were quite relieved.

There was one thing about the army – when a decision was made, there was no messing about. Within a few days all the arrangements had been made and the two craftsmen were off. We'd been together for some time and we had become good friends. But although we were sorry to see them go, there were people coming and going all the time.

By the very nature of the situation, there were changes in personnel taking place on a regular basis so it was something you had become used to. The two craftsmen, who were leaving, were looking forward to a new adventure and once the decision had been made they were ready for off. The two new men would be arriving soon, and we found ourselves wondering what they'd be like, how'd we get on with them, and how would they fit in. It wouldn't be long before we found out.

In due course the two new craftsmen arrived and soon got settled in. They only had a few months to go, so all they were looking forward to was their demobilization (dismissal from service). They were both easy to get on with and we soon became friends. One of them was a cheerful chap with a dry sense of humour. He was always looking forward to payday, and as soon as he got his money he would spend it. However, one day he came up with the idea that he was going to ask the pay corporal how much he was in credit. We found this most amusing because we couldn't understand how he'd worked out that he was in credit at all. But never mind, he went ahead and much to his surprise – and ours as well – he was told he was a few pounds in credit. He should have known that a mistake had been made and despite us telling him to get it checked out, he withdrew the money and spent it. Of course, a short time later the pay corporal sent for him and told him that a mistake had been made that he hadn't been in credit at all.

He had been paid a few pounds more than he was entitled to, so needless to say the army wanted him to pay it back. They were prepared to take it back at so much a week; this was fine until they worked out he didn't have enough time to serve so that he would be able to clear the debt. Then the story goes that they couldn't just stop his pay, that the minimum that they could pay him would be one shilling a day (thirty-five new pence a week). It just shows how money has changed over the years. A youngster today wouldn't thank you for thirty-five pence, not that he could do very much with it anyway.

The chap just took it on the chin, I suppose when you think about it he had scored in the long run. It just meant he would be a bit short for a few weeks. The two of them weren't with us for very long, so they would soon be replaced, which meant getting used to new people once again. It was happening all the time and of course the time was passing, so one day you would be looking forward to demob. Though not for a good while yet, still there was no harm in dreaming.

Very early in our time in Germany, there was a parade called for everyone in the Headquarters Company. We were all assembled in this big hall, wondering what it was all about. In walks this young officer and proceeds to tell us that we would be having a lecture on the consequences of casual sex and the resulting diseases that could be contracted by indulging in these activities. I must admit, we treated the lecture with a great deal of hilarity, especially as the officer giving the lecture couldn't hide his embarrassment and mumbled and stuttered through the whole thing.

CHAPTER SEVENTEEN

Once again, we were off on an exercise for a few days. On returning I found the M.T.O. had bought an old car. As I've said, he was into this sort of thing and this time he'd really surpassed himself – this car was just something else. If you've ever visited a transport museum and seen one of Hitler's or Mussolini's cars, you'll have a good idea what this one was like. The car was big and solid and sat on the road like a tank. The doors would close with a lovely clunk and it had leather seats. I'm pretty sure it was a Horch, a make I had never heard of, and I must admit I've never heard of it since (German car brand founded in 1904 which eventually became Audi in 1985). The engine was unusual, to me anyway. It was a straight eight-cylinder engine with an overhead camshaft – not something I had ever come across in my line of work.

The engine wasn't a runner, so the M.T.O. asked one of the craftsmen to have a look at it to see what he could make of it. The chap decided after checking out the engine that the compressions were poor, so he would have to strip off the cylinder head and sort out the valves. He stripped the cylinder head, got the valves sorted out and started to build it back up again. Then for some reason he took the distributor out. Unfortunately, this caused him problems later on when he got it all back together, as he'd forgotten to take the firing order. He got to the stage of trying to start the engine but wasn't having any joy, so he asked me if I would give a hand, to see if we could sort it out.

During my apprenticeship, I had been attending night school and it had come up about the firing order of an eight-cylinder engine. I don't know why it had come up because as far as I was aware, these engines were few and far between at that time. But anyway, for some unknown reason it had always stuck in my mind, and still does to this day. Another thing in my favour, was the fact that I had spent some time in the engine gang – which meant carrying out the complete overhaul of engines – so I did have some knowledge of them. Having said that, the engines I'd worked on had been pretty run of the mill, nothing compared to this monster.

But nothing ventured, nothing gained, so off we went to see what we could make of the situation. The first thing we did was to make sure we'd got the camshaft set up right. Having done that and been happy we'd got it right, we then fitted the distributor and got the timing set up. Then came the big test – would it start or not?

Fingers crossed, we gave it ago and lo and behold it fired! Off it went much to our delight, plus a little bit of amazement. We got it tuned up and running nicely, so then our thoughts turned to giving it a road test. We couldn't take it outside the camp, so we'd have to think about how we could test it in the camp without running into the R.S.M. By this time the rest of the craftsmen had got involved and we were all looking forward to the road test.

If we'd been caught by any of the officers or the R.S.M., we would most likely have been in trouble. But maybe – just maybe – the fact that the car belonged to the M.T.O., we might have got away with it. Still, it wasn't worth the chance, so we decided to stay in the workshop area. The workshop was situated on the quiet side of the camp near the road we would use.

I must stress that all this work was taking place in our own time; it was a Saturday afternoon, so off we went to spend a pleasant couple of hours enjoying the luxury of the car – and of course we all had to have a go at driving. The car was running well, so we were very pleased with the result and the craftsman handed it over to the M.T.O. with a feeling of a job well done.

I don't know what the M.T.O. did with the car, no doubt he would be thinking that with it being very heavy on petrol not getting many miles to the gallon, it was time to try something else, so the car disappeared and the next thing to appear on the scene was this really big powerful motorbike. I can't remember what it was but it was powerful with a capital 'P'.

Luckily it was a runner, so he asked me to give it the once over and to tune it up. I've mentioned before about the dispatch riders, a couple of them were very taken with this bike so we got it tuned and ready for action.

There was an old disused airfield not too far away from the camp, so the M.T.O. decided we would take it up there to test it out. The M.T.O. – and there was a lieutenant, who was also very keen on motorbikes along with the dispatch riders and me – loaded the bike onto a vehicle and off we went to the airfield.

Once there, the captain had a few practice runs to get the feel of it. When he was satisfied with the machine, he said, 'I'm going to the far end of the runway and I'll see what it can do.' So, he headed off and we saw him turn at the end of the runway, and the next we see he's tearing towards us at over a hundred miles an hour. He did a couple of runs and then he stopped alongside us, and said to me, 'Hop on the back.'

I've got to say here and now that motorbikes have never been my thing. In fact, before I had joined the army, I used to work with a chap who was well over six feet and big with it. Also, he was mad about motorbikes, and he said to me one day, 'Jump on the back and we'll go for a spin.' When we got back to the workshop, he said to me, 'That's the last time I'm taking you on the bike, you were steering it from the back.' So, if I was affecting the bike with the size of him, I thought to myself if that is the case I'll just not bother.

So, I said to the M.T.O., 'Thanks, but there is no way that I'm getting on the back of that bike.' When I told him this, he just laughed and rode off. The lieutenant then had a go and then the two dispatch riders. They all seemed to enjoy themselves, so they were happy.

CHAPTER EIGHTEEN

One of the big occasions during the year for the Worcesters was when they held a big parade on the first of June – The Glorious First of June. This was to celebrate some battle they had been involved in, at some time in the past.

So, the parade ground would come into its own the few weeks before the parade, with all the preparations taking place to make sure that everything would be perfect on the day. The marching would be spot on, all the uniforms would be immaculate and, of course, the boots shining at their best, so that on the day nothing would be left to chance. On the day the battalion was at its best – the band was also part of the parade, so it would turn out to be a day to remember.

One N.C.O. whom I remember in particular, taking a big part in the parade, was the drum major. He was always very smart, marching here, there, and everywhere, but always being at the right place, at the right time.

Strangely enough, our services weren't required on the big day (I've often wondered why), but we got the benefit of being able to watch the whole parade taking place. It was a pleasure for us, without being under the strain that the other lads must have been burdened with. It being a lovely day and a good turnout of spectators, the stage was all set, and we weren't disappointed. The men marching in perfect unison, the band playing away in good style, the parade turned out to be a big success – everyone awed at the sight!

Of course, one of the biggest perks of the day was the special meal that the cooks laid on. The cooks could really turn it on when they had to, so the meal was something to look forward to. I'm sure the men would be very relieved when it was all over as the training for the big event had been going on for weeks, so it would be nice to get back to normality.

The drum major was the N.C.O. in charge of the drummers and buglers in the battalion. While you were in camp the bugle would play a big part in your daily routine. The bugler would sound *Reveille* (morning call), *Cookhouse*, *The Last Post* and of course, *Lights Out*. We knew the buglers quite well, so I think they used to take great delight sounding *Reveille* under our window. There was no way you weren't awake by the time they were finished.

Usually when *The Last Post* was sounded, we would be walking down to the cook house for dinner. At the sound of the first note you would have to stop and stand to attention until it was finished, so it was a tune we knew very well.

One day we were on our way down to dinner, the duty guards were on parade on the square when *The Last Post* started to sound, so we stood to attention. This night, for some reason, the duty bugler got it all wrong and proceeded to make a right hash of the whole thing. Try as he might, the poor chap just couldn't get it right. It was so bad that the duty officer called him across when he'd finished and put him on a charge.

The buglers in the battalion were usually very good, so it must have been a one off. Anyway, I felt sorry for him. But I suppose that the officer had no option than to put him on a charge, as at least they could get to the bottom of what had gone wrong. Ever since then every time I hear *The Last Post* being sounded usually on the TV, I recall this incident and listen intently for any mistakes. The bugler plays a big part in these parades and he's usually on his own with nowhere to hide.

The regiment had a number of horses which were stabled outside the camp. One of the Worcesters was assigned to help look after them. As he mainly lived at the stables and was involved with German staff, it was surprising how quickly he picked up the German language. In a few short weeks he could rattle away in German in good style. They always say that the best way to learn a language is to live with the people, which certainly proved to be true in his case.

Apart from that, he was a bit of a character and was always good for a laugh. One day he was having a meal in the cook house when an officer came around asking people if they had any complaints. He got to this chap and asked him.

'No sir,' he replied, 'I've just eaten them.' A remark which we found to be very funny, but I don't think the officer was too amused.

I did say that I couldn't remember names, which is true, but I was looking at the M.T. Section's photo and he is the one with the white shirt on. How he got away with that, I'll never know. The two of us had a standing joke; every time we met, I would ask him how he was and he would reply, 'Highly salubrious', at which point we would have a good laugh.

CHAPTER NINETEEN

One day the sergeant said to me, 'The M.T.O. wants to see you.'

'What have I done now?' I asked.

'I don't know, you'll have to go and find out,' was the reply.

Off I went to be told the army were holding motorbike trials, the battalion had entered a team, and that I would be the mechanic. I've mentioned before that motorbikes aren't my favourite mode of transport, but it's an order with no questions asked – just get on with it. I was told to go and prepare six bikes and himself, the lieutenant and four of the dispatch riders would make up the team.

A few days later I was told to get a truck, load up the bikes and in a couple of days we would be off. Depending where the trials were being held, you could be away for a while; this particular one, we would be away for three days. The trial was taking place at a camp over a hundred miles away, and not only was I the appointed mechanic, I was also the appointed driver. We got the bikes loaded and ready for the off, I hadn't got a clue where this camp was but the M.T.O. said to follow him.

This was all very well and good but he was driving a Champ (Jeep), while I had this big truck loaded with men and motorbikes. He wasn't noted for hanging about so off he went with me desperately hanging on. However, we managed to arrive at the camp at the same time, much to the relief of the men travelling with me, and of course, to myself – no one was more relieved than me.

At the camp, we were shown our billet and got settled in for the night. The next morning after breakfast, we would head off to where the trials were taking place. There would always be a number of teams entered in the trials, so there was plenty of competition with everyone wanting to do well. The team was doing reasonably, but the M.T.O. was complaining afterwards that his bike wasn't going too well. So, he said to me, 'You had better have a look at it when we get back to camp.'

After the trial we would spend the night at the camp and be ready to depart the next day. I had enjoyed the time on the trials, it was a few days well spent and off course, when we returned to camp a few days to knock off the calendar.

The next morning, we drove out of the camp behind the M.T.O., who immediately shot off down the road. This time we decided to let him go, because we knew the way back to Iserlohn. We drove back at a more leisurely pace, feeling much more relaxed when we arrived this time. I had a look at the M.T.O.'s bike but I couldn't find anything wrong with it, so I got one of the lads to clean it up and park it up ready for the trials.

I must admit that the dispatch riders were very enthusiastic and knew far more about motorbikes than I did. If we had any problems they would soon sort them out, which suited me fine.

We wouldn't have to wait long before there was another trial to go to, with this one being held at Belsen, a name that conjured up all sorts images because of the infamous concentration camp in the area. But we would (maybe) get the chance to have a look around the area and create memories for ourselves. We arrived and were put into our billet once again, a good substantial building with all the amenities, so we weren't roughing it by any means. During the Second World War, as mentioned, there had been a big concentration camp based in Belsen, where a lot of the atrocities during the war had taken place. We'd heard a lot of horror stories about what had taken place there, but we thought that after ten years it would be just like anywhere else. We managed to have a tour around the area but even after all that time you could sense that something awful had taken place there. There was an unpleasant atmosphere about the place. Maybe it was because you'd heard all the stories so you might have been influenced by them. I don't think so, because I didn't like the place, so I don't look back on the trip with any pleasure.

Years later, in 1998, my wife and I did a coach trip, which covered five different European countries. Included in the trip was a visit to Auschwitz. It reminded me of Belsen, it had the same feel and atmosphere. There were twelve different nationalities on the coach, maybe some of them had good reasons for the visit; for me, I didn't find it enjoyable. But maybe there's a good reason for keeping these places in existence, to remind people of the horrors that took place and hope they'll never be repeated in the future.

Back to the trials, which went very well this time, the team put up a good performance. So, everyone was pleased, especially the M.T.O., who arrived back praising me for the work I'd done on the bike. Little did he know! I've often wondered what he'd have said if things hadn't turned out so well. Actually, he was a decent chap, who I got on well with, and I would certainly come across a lot worse than him.

CHAPTER TWENTY

On one particular exercise, we were lying alongside a big open area, when these tanks came thundering towards us. This was an awesome sight, certainly not one I would like to repeat in real live action. Thankful that although they were the enemy for that exercise, we knew they were friendly. Not a consolation that our troops had during the war.

One day, I was driving along when I saw a convoy of tanks coming towards us. The civilian cars were giving them a wide berth and who were we to blame? All of a sudden, one of the tanks did a sharp right turn, shot off the road and finished up between two trees. Luckily without causing any damage to anything or anyone, I can only think that the tank must have developed a fault; I certainly don't think the driver had intended to make the move.

One night, another chap and I were on manoeuvres, when we came across men standing round a fire. We crept up on them and shouted, 'Put your hands up!'

They just laughed and said, 'We've been captured, so go away,' which is what we did, feeling awfully stupid.

A new major arrived at the camp, and according to the grapevine, he was a reservist, who for some reason or other had been recalled to the army. On a couple of occasions, I was ordered to be his driver, which meant driving him around the area, while he would be drawing up plans for exercises that the battalion would be carrying out later in the season. He was a very pleasant chap, easy to get on with, so I enjoyed the time I spent with him. He was quite chatty and we would have some good conversations, but whether the rumours were true about him being recalled, I never found out – that was one thing that he never mentioned.

He would sit overlooking the area where the exercise would be held, to give him a rough idea for his plans. Then, I'm sure, when he got back to camp he would have to finalise everything. The weather on the exercises was generally very good, so it was nice to get away from the workshop for a few days. And of course, when you returned, it was always a few days to tick off your calendar.

The calendar was a homemade effort that I had made when I'd first joined the army. I don't know if it helped to make the time go any faster, probably the opposite. But I suppose, it was nice to see the days getting gradually less and less. If there were a few of the drivers away on leave, I could be called upon to double up as a driver (there were no unions in the army), it was something that you had to accept and get on with.

One time I was down to drive this truck, which meant drawing all the gear that you needed from the company stores. You would have to sign for all the equipment and of course, when you got back to camp it would have to be returned to the stores. One of the items I was issued with was a big camouflage net. This was a huge net and when you stopped for any length of time you and the men you had in the truck would have to cover the truck with this camouflage net. Mainly so any aircraft wouldn't be able to spot you easily. So, this was the first thing on the agenda after you had parked.

For the first few days everything was going fine. We would get to our destination, park the vehicle, and cover it with the camouflage net. The next morning, we would be off again heading for our new destination.

On arrival, we would go through the same procedure until one night I parked the vehicle, gave the men a shout to throw out the net. Much to my disgust it wasn't there, I don't know how but I had lost it. So that meant I could be in trouble on the exercise for not having a net, and then again, even more trouble when I got back to camp. I would be on company orders and have to face up to the consequences.

Not something to look forward to but I only had myself to blame. If I'd had a walk around the truck before I left in the morning, it was so big that I couldn't have missed it. I hadn't done that so it was missing and I would just have to get on with it. I'm sure we'd had word, on this particular exercise, that the Territorial Army could be doing exercises in the area we were in with a possibility of them being dropped in by parachute. All the more reason for having a camouflage net. Luckily, we never saw anyone being dropped by parachute, so I had to be thankful for small mercies.

The next day, on arrival at our overnight stop, I was ordered to do a job before I got set up for the night. Along with the men I set off, we got the job done. By the time we were returning to camp it was dark, so I'm driving along in the dark when I spotted something lying in the ditch. I must have been a couple of hundred yards past when I said to myself, 'That was a camouflage net!'

Much to the consternation of the men in the back, I slammed on the brakes and reversed back. Sure enough, there was a camouflage net lying in the ditch. I hauled it out and with the help of the men got it into the back of the truck. The next morning, I got the chance to have a look at it to find it was a much better net than the one I'd had in the first place. So, I could go back to Iserlohn with a heavy load lifted off my mind. But I knew in my mind that somewhere there would be another poor driver that wouldn't be looking forward to reporting that he'd lost his camouflage net. There were a lot of other regiments in the area involved in the exercise, so it would have been practically impossible to find out who had lost it. I just thanked my lucky stars – you never know, they might have found mine.

On these exercises, we would cover a lot of ground during the day, and on arriving at our destination we would have to set up camp for the night. One of the N.C.O.'s would have the job of drawing up a roster for guard duty, everyone having to take a turn, and they would be on guard for two hours. You would check the list, and make sure you knew where the man after you was sleeping, so that after two hours you could hand it over to him. This sounds quite straight forward but as there were tents dotted all over the place it was quite easy in the dark to make a mistake.

One night, the man on duty found the tent where his relief was sleeping and started banging away trying to wake him up. Unfortunately, he soon found out he'd made a big blunder – it was actually the company sergeant major sleeping there. He wasn't very pleased, to say the least, and told him to go away (or words to that effect). It was the talk of the camp the next day, with the sergeant major having a few more choice words to say to the man, leaving him in no doubt what would happen to him if it ever occurred again.

We were camped in a farming area one night, and one of the men had a small pan. I don't know how but he'd managed to acquire some fat. Earlier in the day we'd had a scout around the area and found a potato field. Once it was dark we went back to the field and borrowed some potatoes, went back to camp, and made some chips. They were very good and we really enjoyed them.

Another time, we had made camp beside a small village, we were preparing to move on when out of one of the farms came two women with small carts loaded with milk churns. The unusual thing about this was that the carts were being pulled by two big dogs. The dogs were all harnessed in, with the women controlling them with a lead. It was the first time I had ever seen this and I've got to say, I've never seen it since. I've often wondered what would have happened if the dogs had spotted a cat. Still I was left to wonder – we were all packed up and ready for off.

On one of the exercises, we would be staying in the same area for a few days. Because of this, tents had been set up with toilets, and a cook house, so we were well set up, it was like a village. The last night, some of the men were allowed to spend a few hours in the small town, which was just a few miles away. Unfortunately, they had gone to the pub in the process, doing some damage. We had a provost corporal; he and his team were more than capable of sorting out any problems. But of course, there was the question of the damage. The next day, I was told to take an officer down to the town and it would be his job to placate the landlord – better him than me!

As we were moving out that day, I was told in no uncertain terms not to mess about, to put my foot down and get back as quickly as possible. So, I was tearing along this road, everything going fine until I went around this bend to be confronted with the sight of dozens of hens right across the road. Before I knew where I was, there were hens scattering everywhere. Whether they all survived or not I don't know, but what I do know is that there were feathers flying everywhere! Needless to say, I kept going.

We got down to the town where the officer proceeded to try and negotiate with the landlord. The damage mustn't have been too bad, as on the offer of some compensation the officer and the landlord came to an amicable arrangement. So, it was off back to the camp. On reflection, after the episode with the hens, I think I decided to go back a different way. I was pleased that we were moving on and couldn't get away fast enough – I had visions of the farmer arriving on the scene looking for the man who'd upset his hens.

On the whole, we seemed to get on quite well with the German people, they just seemed to accept that we were around with no problems. But one day, we were in convoy and we got lost so it meant turning around. The first chance we got was into a farmer's yard. The farmer was standing in the yard and let us know in no uncertain terms that we weren't welcome. He was speaking in German but we got the message.

On one of the exercises, I thought I had landed in trouble big time. They were having a night exercise and I was told I would be this officer's driver for the night. I'm pretty sure I would know all the officers in the battalion, but I didn't recognise this chap at all, so I think he must have been from one of the other regiments. I would be driving him round – we had a signalman in the back – and we started off fine with the officer giving me instructions on the directions I had to take.

He had a map on his knee, which he was reading with a torch, and he told me he told me to carry on along this road and put the torch out. I carried on until I came to this cross road; I looked across at him for directions and he was fast asleep. Now, should I wake him up or should I keep going? He wasn't the most affable of men, so I decided to keep going.

We hadn't gone very far, when I came upon a number of vehicles parked at the roadside, I pulled up behind them and coming towards me was this officer shouting at me in no uncertain terms that me arriving there had ruined the whole exercise, and that I would hear more about it. He hadn't seen the officer sitting beside me, who heard the racket, was awake, but saying nothing.

When he saw the officer with me he calmed down a bit, mainly I think because my officer outranked him. But it was still pretty obvious he was blaming me for the collapse of the exercise. Just then, another officer came along, who turned out to be an umpire, and said, 'You've just been hit by an atomic bomb, so you're all out of the exercise.'

At this, the officer getting on to me walked off muttering to himself. Luckily, I never heard another word about it, so I was thanking my lucky stars. I had visions of finishing up in an army gaol (jail) for the rest of my time, or maybe even longer.

CHAPTER TWENTY-ONE

After a few months in Germany, I was entitled to leave back in the U.K. For the life of me, I cannot remember how I got there and back. I cannot imagine the army paying the fare by any other method than the cheapest, so I think it would be safe to say that I went by boat. As I can't remember anything about the trip, I think it's safe to say that I had an uneventful journey. Having said that, it would have been in the late summer, which would make a big difference from travelling in the middle of winter.

At home, I borrowed a car from a friend of mine, so my wife and I would be able to spend time touring in the Hexham area. Northumberland is a lovely county with plenty of places of interest to see; one of the most famous, and very close to Hexham, is Hadrian's Wall.

In Germany, I was used to driving on the right-hand side of the road, while of course in the U.K. we drive on the left. One day on our travels we were crossing this bridge which was a single lane controlled by traffic lights. I crossed the bridge, but there was no traffic waiting on the other side, so I proceeded to drive up the right-hand side of the road.

It was a long straight road, so I looked into the distance and saw traffic coming towards me.

'Look at that!' I said to my wife. 'Those cars are driving on the wrong side of the road.'

'I don't think so,' said my wife, 'it's you that's on the wrong side of the road.'

Of course, she was right (not an uncommon fact), but it showed me that you had to be extra careful, as it just took a split second to make a wrong move, the results of which could have been disastrous.

We had a nice couple of weeks together but as usual, the time passed all too quickly, and before I knew it, the leave was over and it was time to return to camp. In Germany, we drove on the right-hand side of the road, but what made it even more awkward was the fact that the vehicles we were driving were designed for the U.K., which meant you as the driver would be sitting driving along the roadside verge. The biggest problem with this was when you were wanting to overtake. A manoeuvre which was most difficult, if not practically impossible, as you had to be nearly on the wrong side of the road before you would have a clear view. Luckily you would be very seldom on your own, so you would always get help from your passenger.

One day, I was sitting passenger-side in a truck with two vehicles in front of us. The truck in front pulled out to overtake and the driver that I was with just followed him. When the driver in front pulled back onto his own side and the road cleared, there's this truck heading straight towards us. There was violent evasive action on the part of both drivers and how we missed each other I still don't know. I lost one of my nine lives in that moment and my heart was going like the hammers for some time after.

CHAPTER TWENTY-TWO

Most of the men in the battalion came from the same area, and a lot of them would have known each other before they had joined the forces. We were all very friendly getting on well together so that there wasn't a lot of trouble.

The M.T.O. had a driver and a batman – these two got on very well together and were the best of pals. That is until one day they fell out, over I'm sure something quite trivial, and a fight ensued. The next day we were on parade with the M.T.O. (followed by an N.C.O.) walking along the lines, looking everyone up and down. He stops at his driver, takes a look at his face, and says, 'What happened to you?'

The driver was a chap with a ready wit and never beat for an answer said, 'I walked into a door, sir!'

The M.T.O. gave him a look and carried on, got to his batman, took one look at him, and said, 'I suppose you walked into the same door?' While this was going on, we were watching the drama unfold, all thinking it was very funny and had to laugh to ourselves, of course.

One thing in particular that I remember about this driver, was that every time he stopped his vehicle, before switching off the engine, he would give the engine a big rev. His theory was, and I must admit it's a theory I've heard before, that it made for easier starting when you fired the engine up again. He'd taken this knowledge to heart, so that's what he did. It didn't matter where, especially in a convoy, you would always know where he was. One day, one of the drivers came down to the workshop and told us he'd had a disagreement with one of the M.T. corporals and they'd really fallen out. He wasn't a happy man at all.

The phone rang in the workshop office and the R.E.M.E. sergeant shouted to this driver that the M.T.O. wanted to speak to him on the phone. The driver, thinking it was the corporal, picked up the phone and shouted to the person on the other end, assuming it's not the M.T.O. at all, 'Go and get lost!' (or once again words to that effect), and slammed down the phone. Unfortunately, he'd made a big mistake – it was the M.T.O. on the phone. He wasn't pleased, to say the least.

Immediately the phone rang again, for the sergeant to be told, 'To get that man up to my office, right away!'

The driver reported to the M.T.O. and had to try and explain what had happened, how he thought it was the corporal having a joke. This didn't stop him from getting a right row but I think the M.T.O. saw the funny side of it and let the whole thing drop.

On the odd occasion during this period, I would have to go down to an American camp, which wasn't too far away. I would have to report to their workshop and after I'd sorted out what I'd gone there for one of them would take me to their canteen. You would notice the difference straight away, they had a far greater variety of food than us. The biggest difference was the quality of their uniforms, which were much superior to ours. Probably the reason that I was there in the first place was to borrow something. Our uniforms were thick and heavy and not that comfortable to wear. My main gripe was about the greatcoat. I absolutely hated the thing – it was heavy and another reason why I didn't like it was because it hung on me like a sack.

One time we were all called upon to parade in front of the quartermaster and we would have to wear greatcoats. The quartermaster, who was a captain, walked along the lines checking everyone and making a comment here and there. He took one look at me and told me to report to the stores and get that greatcoat changed for something that fits. That was fine, it was a better fit, but it didn't improve the quality. One drawback was that the buttons on the new coat were for the regiment, so I had to set them too and change them, which was a bit of a bind.

CHAPTER TWENTY-THREE

It was getting near to Xmas time, so our thoughts were turning to what time we would get off. We would get leave but we wouldn't be entitled to a pass home. If we wanted to go home, we would have to pay our own fare. Otherwise it would be a case of spending the time round the camp, not something to look forward to. Four of us made enquiries and found out we would be able to get a flight from Dusseldorf to London.

My wife, who was working and making more money than me at the time, suggested she would send me the money. As I was an employee of British Rail, I was entitled to a free pass from London to Inverness, where we would be spending the Xmas and New Year holidays; another of the reasons why I could afford the trip. The four of us went ahead and booked the flights, so it was a case of the time passing and we would be off. We set off for Dusseldorf and booked the plane. We boarded the plane, at that time it was a prop plane. This would be my first flight and even though it rattled along, I was happy.

Arriving in London, I made my way to the railway station to board a train for Inverness; at that time the journey was long and slow. Not like today, where the train journeys have been cut dramatically with new technology. Still, I was thankful to have got the leave and to be able to make the journey. There were plenty of people left behind in the camp who couldn't afford to do it, so I was one of the lucky ones.

I enjoyed my stay in Inverness. It's a lovely part of Scotland, but as usual the time passed too quickly, so it was back on the train heading for London.

One of my travelling companions actually came from London, and his family lived there. So, we'd made arrangements that on the way back the three of us would stay the night with his family. He'd drawn up a plan giving me directions on how to find his home – a bit daunting in a place like London, but the directions were good, and I found the house no bother. This chap was a very good cricketer and played for Worcestershire, most likely that being the reason for him being in the regiment in the first place.

Whether he ever made it to the first team, I don't know, but while he was in Germany, he would often be away playing in some competition or other. We stayed the night with his family and they were very good to us. The next morning it was an early start and we would be off to the airport to catch the flight back to Dusseldorf, and then back to Iserlohn.

I was still keeping my diary up to date, ticking off the days. I was well into my second year but the days just seemed to pass slowly. Not like now, the older you get, the faster they seem to go.

CHAPTER TWENTY-FOUR

We were well into the throes of winter, with a lot of snow on the ground. This was ideal for holding winter sports, which is what the army were about to do in a place aptly named Winterberg. Of course, the regiment had entered a team.

They wouldn't be taking a lot of transport, so they didn't take an R.E.M.E. craftsman with them, which was a good idea as far as I was concerned. I'd heard they were sleeping in tents, which in wintry conditions didn't seem ideal to me. But as fate often has it, I wouldn't have to wait long before I found out for myself what the conditions were like, as I left for Winterberg.

A couple of days before, I was summoned to the M.T.O.'s office to be told they'd had word from the ski team that one of their vehicles was causing problems. The M.T.O. said I would have to go to Winterberg to see if I could sort out the problem.

This didn't seem like a good idea to me; it was the middle of winter with snow goodness knows how deep on the ground, and to crown it all, they were sleeping in tents. But there wasn't any point in protesting, orders are orders. There was a ration truck going up to Winterberg the next day, so I went back to the workshop and got my tools together ready for the off.

The next day we set off, Winterberg was a long drive from Iserlohn, the nearer we got to Winterberg the deeper the snow became. The road conditions were getting worse by the minute, but at least we were sitting in a truck with the luxury of it having doors. We'd set off from Iserlohn early and didn't arrive in Winterberg until late in the afternoon. By the time we reached there, it was starting to get dark, so I wouldn't have time to look at the vehicle. It would be a case of finding my sleeping quarters and getting settled in for the night. Each tent would have about ten beds in it with a stove in the middle. You would be fine huddled up next to the stove, but move a couple of feet away, and the cold would hit you.

At night there would be a special guard on duty, it was their job to keep the tents free from ice. They were armed with long poles so that if ice formed on the tents they would be able to knock it off. You wouldn't get much sleep at the best of times, without hearing someone battering away at the tent. This was one time I was pleased to use my greatcoat, putting it on top of my blankets; not that it made much difference, I don't remember having a pleasant night.

The ski team were enjoying themselves, they would be away from the camp all day, while the non-skiers were getting the chance to have a go on the skis, some of them finding out they were quite good. I did hear one of the drivers had been entered in the team because one of the team was injured and they were a man short. So, from not being able to ski when he had arrived there, it seems he had done quite well for the team. The next morning, it was up early finding the wash tent, having a wash and shave, then going for breakfast. After that it was off to find the vehicle with the problem.

It was so cold that you were ordered to wear your greatcoat. In fact, if you were caught not wearing it, you would be put on a charge. As I've said before, I found this coat uncomfortable to wear, and the idea of me trying to repair this vehicle in these conditions didn't impress me at all. I had a word with the driver and got his report on the problem with the vehicle. I had a look at it and took it for a test run, where I concluded I wouldn't be able to repair it on the spot and the best thing to do would be to take it back to Iserlohn. They would have the parts I would need and I could repair it there.

In my judgement, I would be able to get it back to Iserlohn, hopefully without a problem. Having decided that was the best course of action, there was no reason for me to hang about Winterberg. I could be off back to Iserlohn and as the day was still young I would be back at a reasonable time. So off I went to find the officer in charge of the team, so I could tell him what I had found and what needed to happen.

AUSTIN CHAMP.

IT WAS ONE OF THESE VEHICLES THAT WAS

HAVING TROUBLE IN WINTERBERG.

Figure 11. Austin Champ. It was one of these vehicles that was having trouble in Winterberg. 1955

I found the team commander accompanied by the company sergeant major, made my report on what I had found and what I considered the best course of action. I can still remember the C.S.M. scowling in the background, probably thinking how could I have the audacity to tell the major what course of action would be the best to take.

Having said that, the major considered what I'd said and agreed with me, I saluted and turned to go ready to go back to the tent, get my gear and be off. Or at least that's what I had in mind when he stopped me and said, 'Just hang on, I've got my car in a garage in Dortmund for repair and it will be ready tomorrow. You can stay here tonight and tomorrow you can take me to Dortmund.'

I didn't want to stay another night, but what could I do but agree, so I saluted again and once again turned to leave. He called me back again and shouted, 'IF WE BREAK DOWN YOU HAD BETTER LOOK OUT!' So, on that cheerful note I left him and returned to my tent. It was going to be another night under canvas for me – what a thought!

However, it turned out to be a nice day, I got the opportunity to have a look around the area and to watch some of the skiers in action. I've never been a skier myself but I could see they were enjoying themselves, seeing why it's such a popular sport. Not my cup of tea I'm afraid, especially when I stood at the bottom of a ski jump; when you look at it from below, it puts the fear of death in you. The people who get involved in the sport must have nerves of steel. Standing there, I could just imagine them hurling themselves into space. Having said that, I'm sure that hours and hours of practice would have gone into them developing their skills. The day soon passed and I would spend another cold night in the tent, but at least with the thought that it would be my last night there.

Up next morning, I went through the usual routine – off for breakfast, went to pick up the vehicle, got it started and off to pick up the major. I forgot to mention that when he was telling me the day before about me taking him to Dortmund, he had said, 'You make sure you know the way to Dortmund!'

Not only had I to contend with the possibility of the vehicle breaking down, I would also have to make sure that we didn't get lost. Still, I would just have to deal with these problems if they happened. The roads were treacherous and that's an understatement. They were thick with ice and not a drop of sand or grit in sight.

The vehicle we had was an Austin Champ; these machines had a canvas roof, but unfortunately, they didn't have any doors and it was absolutely freezing. However, I've got to say that it was the one time I was pleased to wear my greatcoat, probably the only time during my army service.

The officer was sitting there, not making any comments or having any conversation, when all of a sudden, he said, 'Could you not drive any faster?' I was driving at what I considered to be a reasonable speed for the conditions.

'Well, sir,' I said, 'I reckon that if I drive any faster there's a good chance we'll finish up in the ditch, we'll be lucky if we get to Dortmund in one piece.'

Anyway, after a long, hairy, and silent journey, we arrived in Dortmund. I found the garage and waited until he made sure that his car was ready. It was, so off I went back to Iserlohn and believe me, I was pleased to get back to camp. I'm sure I was cold for a week after this trip. I did hear later that after collecting his car, the officer had started back to Winterberg. On the way he had slid off the road, I don't know if he'd caused much damage but I'm afraid that I didn't have much sympathy for him.

CHAPTER TWENTY-FIVE

Attached to the regiment was a Royal Medical Corp. captain, he was the battalion doctor. We found him to be a very decent chap. As far as we were concerned, being attached to our regiment made him one of us. If we met him he would always pass the time of day and have a few words in the passing.

During the summer, it wouldn't be very often that the five of us would be in the camp together. But this particular day we were all walking down to the cook house for our evening meal.

As we got to the square *The Last Post* started to sound, we all stopped and stood to attention. Away in front of us was the doctor, and after *The Last Post* had sounded, we started off walking again. As we got near to the doctor, one of the lads said something funny, which made us all laugh. When we got to the doctor because we weren't wearing berets you didn't have to salute; what you did in this situation was to brace yourself to attention and turn your head to the officer, which is what we did and carried on, not thinking another thing about it. However, we did hear later on the grapevine that the doctor was convinced we had been laughing at him, and our source of information reckoned he wasn't pleased, to say the least.

Now for him to think that couldn't have been further from the truth. The remark that the chap had made was a spontaneous remark and nothing to do with the doctor at all. But it wasn't hard to tell that something had upset him because when we met after that, he certainly wasn't the same. In the end we decided that a couple of us would go across to the officer's mess hall to see him and to explain what had happened.

Myself and another craftsman went across to see him, but it didn't matter how hard we tried we just couldn't get through to him at all. It had certainly got to him and nothing we could say would convince him otherwise. In the end, we could only apologise once again and accept that we were getting nowhere. We would just have to leave it at that. Before, when we would have contact with him, we could have a laugh and a joke but that all changed – he was never the same, which was a pity, but life is like that sometimes.

The Headquarters Company Commander was a major, who had his family with him, so they lived in married quarters outside the camp. One day, he said to one of the other craftsmen and me that he was having trouble with his car, and could we have a look at it for him. It was parked up at his house, so he suggested it would be best if we went there to carry out the repairs. We agreed to this and as we usually got the Saturday afternoons off, we would be there on the following Saturday to do the job.

The major and his wife had a young boy, who was just starting to talk, and they had a nanny, who helped look after the boy. She was German, so she would speak to the boy in German, when he was talking to his mother and father he would speak in English. He would be watching us, working and chatting away in English, but then he would trot across to the garden fence. As the German people passed they would stop and have a chat with him and he would be answering in German, no bother. It didn't matter to him what language he spoke, it came naturally to him. I should imagine that if he kept it up it would be a very useful skill to have as he got older.

Some of the younger officers would buy themselves a second-hand car. They usually needed a bit of work on them, but that wouldn't put them off. They seemed to like pottering about on them. One of the lieutenants had got this car, and he asked me if he could borrow some tools. I lent him the tools and I would get them back after the weekend.

On the Monday, the first thing I did was go to the barber shop to get a haircut. The barber had a room where he did the hair cutting and a waiting room next door. I was sitting next in line waiting my turn with two other chaps sitting beside me, when in walks this officer that had borrowed the tools from me. On one of his fingers was this huge bandage, the sight of which, caused me and the other two to smile. This didn't go down well with the officer, and to make matters worse, we hadn't stood up when he entered the room. He started shouting at the other two lads for not standing, when an officer entered the room, threatening to put them on a charge. Whether he ever did or not I don't know.

But he never said a word to me; I think this was one of the times that doing someone a favour paid off. Probably what had annoyed him the most was us smiling at the sight of his finger. Although he was right, you always had to stand up when an officer entered the room. On reflection, I'm sure he jumped the queue.

CHAPTER TWENTY-SIX

Generally, we wouldn't have to attend parades, but every now and again either the company commander or the M.T.O. would put out an order for everyone to attend. I had been issued with a Sten gun – a semi-automatic weapon – so on this day I would have to parade with my Sten gun on the Battalion Square. First of all, there would be the inspection, which would be followed by drill, in this particular case, taken by the company sergeant major. We were marching along, in good style, when he called us to a halt, he came straight over to me and snapped, 'You! You would think that you hadn't been on parade since your boy service!'

Boy service! I said to myself, *Boy service, what boy service?!* I didn't want to be in the army at all, so I don't know where he got the boy service idea from. By the way, I've written what he said politely; they could really let rip with no punches pulled, not leaving you a leg to stand on. Anyway, just as he was getting into full swing, he spotted someone else doing something he didn't like and shot off to sort him out, luckily forgetting about me in the process. As I say I didn't go on parade very often so I must have been a bit rusty, that's my excuse anyway.

Not long after this the M.T.O. called for everyone to attend his normal morning parade, and to take our weapons ready for inspection. Along comes the M.T.O., followed by the usual N.C.O. I don't mean a particular N.C.O., just that they would always be followed by an N.C.O., whose job it would be to take a note of anything the M.T.O. didn't like and what he wanted done about it. He walked along the lines, got to me, stopped, looked me up and down and said, 'There's dust on your Sten gun.' Turned to the N.C.O. and said, 'Put this man on a charge.'

At the end of the parade, I had to go and see the N.C.O. and tell him I couldn't report to the company commander as I was going out of the camp for the next few days. I thought he might have said forget about it, but no, I would have to report when I got back. The motorcycle team were entered in another competition, so I would be off for the next few days.

We spent a few pleasant days at the trials, everyone enjoying the experience, and the M.T.O. having a dig now and again, saying I had something to look forward to when I got back to camp. I'm sure alluding to the fact that I would be on company orders, no doubt letting me know he hadn't forgotten about it. When we got back to camp and I checked company orders, sure enough my name was down to report the next day.

The next day, I reported to the company office along with a few others, who were also on a charge. We would all have to appear before the company commander. We were standing there waiting to be called in one at a time, but before it got started the lieutenant – who had been with us on the motorcycle trials – came in and went into the company office. He was in there for a few minutes, then out he came. He didn't speak but he gave me a nod in the passing.

I was called in. I say 'called in', but actually I was marched in, at the double, by the company sergeant major. Called to a halt in front of the company commander, who proceeded to ask me why I had turned up on parade with dust on my Sten gun.

You couldn't just stand there saying nothing, you'd have to think of a reason, no matter how feeble. Not that I thought that they would take much notice, but you had to try. So, I said, 'Sir, the only reason I can think of is that I'd cleaned the gun ready for inspection and after that, the floor of the room had been swept.' And I was sure that was how the dust had got onto my Sten gun.

I could see that my explanation had fallen on deaf ears when he proceeded to tell me that he took a dim view of the situation. Then he gave me a right rollicking, not leaving me a leg to stand on. I thought to myself, *I'm in for a few days jankers here, there's no way that he's going to let me off.*

But I was wrong, thank goodness, he carried on to say that as it was my first offence, he was going to admonish me but not to let it happen again, as he wouldn't be so lenient the next time. I heaved a big sigh of relief, saluted, did an about-turn, and was marched out at the double. Somehow, I don't think my explanation made much of an impression. It was more than likely that the lieutenant had put in a word for me, probably instigated by the M.T.O., and that had been the reason for me getting off.

Having to do jankers, reporting to the guardroom morning and night, and doing jobs about the camp, didn't appeal to me at all, so I had been very lucky. The only other time I was on company orders for what you would call a chargeable offence, was for something far more serious.

The workshop where we carried out the repairs was situated to one side of the camp. Although there was a road past there, everyone using it would stop at the workshop. No one used the road at the other side of the workshop. Anyway, that's what I thought, but what happened just shows how wrong you can be, and that you should never take anything for granted.

I had to fit a new winch rope to one of the vehicles. So, I hooked the rope onto another truck and started to wind it on to the winch. Unfortunately, I had the rope stretched across the road and I was lying under the truck that I was fitting the rope to. Unknown to me, along the road from the quiet side came a motorbike ridden by a sergeant.

All of a sudden, the truck that I was lying under lifted up at the back and the rear wheels came down on my foot. Luckily the way my foot was lying, the heel of my boot took most of the weight. The motorbike had run into the rope, the bike stopped but the sergeant didn't – he shot off up the road!

I finished up with bruising to my foot, while the sergeant had done some damage to his legs. Looking back on it, we were both very lucky, the consequences could have been much more serious. Nevertheless, we were both hobbling around the camp for a few days. The accident had caused some damage to the bike as well, so the incident had to be reported. With the result that once again I was on company orders.

You would have to go through the usual palaver of getting dressed up in your best B.D. and, of course, your boots bulled to perfection. Then present yourself at company office, to face the company commander. The sergeant was also on parade, I was called in first and asked to explain what had happened, which I did.

I finished my report and was told to wait in the corridor so the sergeant major marched me out. Then the sergeant was called into the office to put his side of the story to the major. After a few minutes, I was called back into the office and asked if the bike could be repaired. I'd had a look at it and decided that there wasn't a lot of damage to it and that it could be repaired. So, I told the major that it could, he told me to carry on, so that's what I did. Officially, I never heard another word about it, but the sergeant, who was a decent bloke, kept me informed.

Another accident that I had – or maybe I should call it a near miss – happened when I was working on an Oxford Carrier, which is a tracked vehicle. These vehicles had very heavy metal sides which were hinged; if you dropped the sides, it gave you easier access to the engine. I had a driver helping me, we loosened the catches, and I told the driver to hold on until I went and got something. I'd just turned and took a step away when he let the side go. It scraped down my back, luckily it didn't hit me full force, but the air was very blue when I told him what I thought of him. I've been bothered with a bad back over the years, so probably this didn't help matters any.

I used to quite enjoy driving these carriers, and there was an area very close to the camp, which was suitable for testing them out. They didn't have a steering wheel, and you would steer them using levers; it was different but you soon got used to it. What was surprising, was what variation in equipment the battalion had, so it was interesting and also gave you the chance to develop new skills, working on machines that you'd never worked on before.

CHAPTER TWENTY-SEVEN

Time was passing and the battalion would be starting to prepare once again for the big parade – The Glorious First of June. Headquarters company were all called out on parade with no exceptions, and we would all have to attend. So, there we were, marching up and down with the rest, when the sergeant called us to a halt and told this chap to fall out. He then got the chap to march on his own. Of course, we were all watching what was going on. We had to laugh, he was marching along swinging his right arm and his right leg together. Then his left arm and left leg together. The correct way is to swing your right arm and left leg, then your left arm and right leg.

When you would be doing your initial training, this would happen quite often, you would see a lot of men making this mistake. But to see a man, who had been through all his training and had been in the army for some time, was just unbelievable. The sergeant wasn't amused at all but we found it to be very funny. The sergeant called some of the other N.C.O.s over to see the performance, they just laughed and shook their heads. No doubt the chap would have to receive some extra attention to bring him into line.

As we wouldn't be participating on the big day, our services after the first parade wouldn't be required. The practising would go on for weeks to make sure everyone was up to scratch and ready for the big day. We would be able to see it all as spectators, having a ringside seat. As usual, the day went with a swing; everything was going to plan and everyone was happy with the results. Of course, there was always the slap-up meal to look forward to.

CHAPTER TWENTY-EIGHT

In this chapter, I would like to write about the opportunities I had to visit some of the memorable places in Germany that I found to be well worth a visit.

During the Second World War, one of the targets highlighted by The Royal Air Force were the dams in the Ruhr Valley. These dams held the water needed to supply the factories in the valleys and also for the operation of the power stations. The problem for the R.A.F. was that the Germans had the dams so well fortified, that it would be difficult, if not impossible, for the R.A.F. to get anywhere near them.

One of the dams causing them concern was the Möhne Reservoir. A chap by the name of Barnes Wallace was given the task of designing a bomb that was capable of having a reasonable chance of succeeding in carrying out the task. He considered the situation and concluded that nothing less than a direct hit would have the desired effect. Dropping the bombs into the water wouldn't cause damage to the dam wall, so he would have to look for another method. What he came up with was, the now famous, Bouncing Bomb and this bomb would be dropped by the squadron, who subsequently became known as the Dam Busters.

Now the problem for the R.A.F. was that to try and get anywhere near the dam wall they would come under very heavy fire, thus having a very slim chance of succeeding with their mission. Plus, the fact that they would more than likely incur very heavy losses, which was something they would want to avoid.

The bomb that Barnes Wallace had designed would be dropped a distance away from the wall and it would bounce across the top of the water, like a stone. On hitting the dam wall, it would explode breaching the wall, allowing the water through and flooding the valley below. The mission turned out to be successful causing major problems for the Germans.

I'm no expert on the subject, but there have been books written and films made about the Dam Busters and their exploits. The reason I've given a short summary of the story is because it came up on the notice board that a trip had been organised to go and visit the Möhne Reservoir. I was all for this, a good day away, with something in my opinion that would be well worth seeing.

We drove through very pleasant countryside enjoying the scenery until we came to the dam. Approaching the dam, all you would see was this big expanse of water with the dam in the distance. It wasn't until you walked down to the dam that you realised how enormous it was. When you viewed it from the top and then walked down into the valley, looking up you could well see what devastation would be caused, when it was breached. The valley would be flooded for miles, though I did read the Germans had the dam operational again in a very short time.

There was a road across the dam, which you could walk across with souvenir shops, so you could buy a memento to remind you of your trip. We had a good day, the dam was well worth seeing, and I've got to say, a great engineering feat to build it in the first place.

Speaking of memorable places, the battalion had managed to be allocated tickets for a Louis Armstrong concert, so anyone interested could put their name down. I was all for this, put my name down and was allocated a ticket and a seat on the bus. The concert was to be held in Dusseldorf, in a huge cycling arena. You could just imagine big cycling events that had been held there.

A full house was expected, so the centre of the arena was filled with seats. Louis Armstrong was a world-famous artist, with an excellent backing band, so it was packed; there wasn't an empty seat in the hall. Louis Armstrong was instantly recognisable by his unusual voice but apart from that, he was a brilliant musician, so it was a night to remember, particularly his rendering of *Hello Dolly* – one of my favourites – a song that he had made very much his own. I had a good seat very near the front, so I had a clear view of everything that went on, he was very much a showman, he and his band came across very well, really enjoyable.

One of the exercises was to be held around the Wuppertal area. I knew before we left that the city was well known for having an overhead railway. But knowing about it and being prepared for it, were two different things. Driving up the main street and looking up to see a train coming towards you, was quite frightening the first time you experienced it. We were based in the area for a few days, so I did get the opportunity to travel on the train. The platforms were high up so there were a lot of steps to climb, but it was well worth seeing and travelling on. It was certainly unique, and I'm not positive, but it might have been the only one in the world at that time.

Another trip that I had was with some trepidation as it was to war graves in the area, but it was something I felt I had to do. This was very sad and humbling, to see hundreds of gravestones laid out in neat rows but I must admit, well looked after, with the number, rank and name of the serviceman on the headstone. Their age brings tears to your eyes. A lot of them were in their teens, every one holding the story of the loss of a young life, with the grief and suffering left behind for the families. The old saying that time is a great healer somehow doesn't seem to me to apply in these circumstances. But the one thing that applies to us all, is 'NEVER FORGET'.

CHAPTER TWENTY-NINE

There were other regiments based around Iserlohn; it was a nice town, not too big, surrounded by lovely countryside. Our camp was on the outskirts of town, so it was just a good walk to the town centre. Because of the large number of troops based in the area, there was an excellent cinema in the town centre, with all the latest films being shown. So, one of our regular haunts at the weekend would be the cinema.

There was a big N.A.A.F.I. in the town who did good meals. That would be our first port of call and then it would be off to the cinema. One night at the cinema, I heard someone shouting my name. Now in my two years of national service, I only ever met two people from my hometown. The first was the sergeant from the training camp in Honiton, the second was this chap giving me a shout at the cinema. It was nice to see him and to catch up with all the news. Although, I've just remembered he told me that another chap from the hometown was in a hospital not too far away, so I made a point of paying him a visit.

During my time with the Worcesters, I had been involved in a lot of sporting activities. Mostly I played football, we played a lot of matches against other companies and against other regiments in the area. These matches would always be very competitive, everyone wanting to win. It was quite possible, when I was in the camp, for me to be playing football a couple of times a week.

The photograph below is of the team entered in the six a side competition by the M.T. Section. There were a lot of teams entered, so there were a few rounds to play. I cannot remember if we won or not but we must have done pretty well, especially as the man in the photo, in the white collar, is the company sergeant major. He must have been the referee, he's all smiles in the photo but he was another man that it was best not to tangle with.

Having said that it was their job to maintain discipline, as long as you respected that, you would get on fine. There was no doubt that if they had shown the slightest weakness, somebody would be ready to exploit it, so they made sure everybody would know where they stood, and respect them for it.

PHOTOGRAPH OF THE M.T. SECTIONS SIX A SIDE TEAM.

Figure 12. Photograph of the M.T. Sections six a side team. Author Top 2nd left, 1955

One day the sergeant major sent for me and said, 'I'm putting you into the hockey team, you'll be playing this afternoon.' So, if that's what he said, that's what you did, even though I had never played a game of hockey in my life. In the afternoon I turned up and played the game and thoroughly enjoyed it, so I played quite often after that.

Most of the sporting activities would take place during the winter months, as of course during the other months we would be away from the camp carrying out the training exercises.

In the camp, they had this huge gymnasium, well equipped, and well used by the battalion. Although, I must say it wasn't a place we would spend much time in. We always had plenty of work to do, so it wouldn't be very often that we would get the chance to use the gym. However, the battalion had a very enthusiastic boxing team, who we would see about the camp. Especially when they were in training for an Inter-Regimental Boxing competition. This was to be held in the gymnasium, as they had a boxing ring in the centre of the gym, with seats all round.

On the night of the competition, there was a big buzz in the gym, with every seat taken and everyone looking forward to the event. We wouldn't be disappointed; as far as I remember, it was a very close contest with everyone enjoying a good night.

One of the regular events with the battalion was the cross-country runs. I wouldn't enter them all but if I got the chance I would go on them, as it was something that I really enjoyed. You'll see from the photo that the countryside around Iserlohn was ideal for such activities.

The back wall of the workshop was covered from side to side with windows, looking out over the Iserlohn countryside. If I wasn't on the run, I could look out of the window and see the start of the race, see the runners leaving the camp and heading off through the trees and up the hill. Now cross-country running is not everyone's cup of tea, a few of the wide boys would duck under cover and hide among the trees. They would sit there and have a smoke, until the runners started to return and then they would join back in.

VIEW OVERLOOKING ISERLOHN.

Figure 13. View overlooking Iserlohn. 1955

They weren't stupid, they would wait until most of the runners were passed before they re-joined the run. Let's face it if they had got back too near the front they might have found themselves in the battalion cross-country team – that would never do! As far as I know, they got away with it, as the workshop was probably the only vantage point on the camp where you could see what was going on. There were only a few that did it, they obviously enjoyed their smoke more than they enjoyed the run.

The commanding officer of the battalion was a lieutenant-colonel, and whenever you saw him about the camp, he would be followed by his entourage. Not that I ever had much contact with him; I did have a look at his car a couple of times but I'm sure I would receive the order to do so from a third party. However, he had his family with him living in married quarters. He had a son who was about ten, whose idea of entertainment was to come down to the workshop and give us cheek from a distance. All a bit of fun really, we would give as good as we got.

One time we were washing this truck outside the workshop, when along comes the colonel's son and of course, as usual, he starts giving us cheek. The chap with the hose turned it on him with the result that he was soaked. From the workshop we could see across the square, and that day, who's coming across the square followed by his usual entourage, is the colonel himself. As soon as the boy sees his father, he's off like a shot shouting, 'Those men over there turned a hose on me and I'm soaking wet!' By this time, we were hiding around the corner, but we could hear and see what was going on.

'Well,' said the colonel, 'What were you doing?'

'I wasn't doing anything!' Cried the boy.

'A likely story, go home and get dried and try and behave yourself in future.'

Either the colonel had a sense of humour or he had too much on his mind that day to be bothered with his son's plight. Either way we were off the hook. Needless to say, the boy was back within a few days, everything back to normal.

CHAPTER THIRTY

Although the Second World War had been over for ten years, I'm pretty sure we were still classed as being on active service. During my time it was announced that this would be lifted and the Germans were able to start forming their own armed forces.

It wasn't long before you would start to see uniformed soldiers on the streets. It was quite funny, as you would see German soldiers walking towards you. It didn't matter what rank you were, in fact a uniform would do. They would salute. A situation which we found very funny but we were ordered not to salute back.

The next exercise that I would be on was to a place called Putlos, which is on the Baltic and the exercises were to last for six weeks. So, all being well this would take a big chunk out of my remaining time in the army. As we would be away for so long, we would be preparing for some time, getting all our gear together and ready for the off.

Putlos was a long journey from Iserlohn, so we would be travelling most of the day before we would arrive. We arrived at the camp to discover it was a permanent camp, so the conditions were good. We could look forward to a comfortable stay.

It was a lovely area, so with the weather being excellent all during my stay, it was an enjoyable time. There wasn't a fence around the camp, so you were free within reason to come and go as you pleased. The days would be taken up with the exercises but at night you would have the opportunity to go out of camp and explore the area.

There was a workshop on the camp that I would spend most of the day working in, they also had a workshop employing local mechanics. If I was stuck for anything I found them very helpful, they would do their best to try and help you out.

Maybe this easy access to the camp turned out to be not such a good idea. As on the third morning we were there, they had to hold an identification parade. The story goes that the night before, a German had been attacked and hit over the head with a fence post. Whether this was true or not I don't know, but they definitely held the parade because I can remember seeing the German walking along the lines escorted by an officer. Seemingly the one thing that the German could remember was that whoever had attacked him wore a hackle in his beret. A hackle is a plume of feathers worn on the beret in order to honour some battle that the regiment had been involved in away in the past.

A lot of regiments wear the hackle, so as there were at least men from two regiments staying at the camp, he wouldn't have an easy job trying to identify the man who'd attacked him. There would be about two hundred men on parade, the only difference in the hackle between regiments is the colour. As far as I could gather he didn't manage to identify anybody. Fortunately, I didn't wear the hackle so my attendance wasn't required. Things must have settled down after that, as I didn't hear of any further trouble during the six weeks that we were there.

In the battalion, there was a section of Anti-Tank guns, attached to them there was a R.E.M.E. armourer. I'm pretty sure he had a room within the armoury, so work wise we wouldn't have a lot of contact, but socially he would mix with us and we were all very friendly.

One of the main reasons for us going to Putlos was that it was the ideal place for carrying out practices with these guns. As the armourer was heavily involved with their maintenance, he was up in Putlos with us. Before we had left Iserlohn, one of the guns had been sent to a workshop for repairs that couldn't be carried out at the camp. However, they were hoping to hear from the workshop that it was ready and that we could go and collect it.

In due course, word came through that it was ready for collection. I would have to go for it, so I got hold of an Austin Champ, and the armourer and I set off to collect it. The workshop was a good distance away, and even though we started off early, it would be late in the evening before we would get back to camp.

It was well into the afternoon by the time we got to the workshop, the armourer getting the paperwork sorted and us ready for the return journey. We were still a fair distance from Putlos and it was starting to get dark. I put on the lights and thought I'd better stop to check if the lights were working on the gun. You've guessed it, the lights on the gun weren't working, so here we were stuck miles away from anywhere. What do I do? It was a case of trying to sort out the problem or carrying on and hoping for the best.

Some electrical faults can take a while to find and it's not to say that I would have any spares with me. There wasn't a lot of traffic on the road, so I decided, in my wisdom, that I would carry on, which proved to be a big mistake. I hadn't gone a mile when a police car came up behind flashing his lights for us to stop.

I said to the armourer, 'That's us in trouble, we're liable to be arrested.' I think I'd better rephrase that *I* would be arrested, after all I was the driver. They could speak no English, and we couldn't speak German but at least they were smiling so we hoped that was a good sign.

We managed to convey to them, by pointing and using hand signals, where we were heading. Although looking back I'm sure they would know the area well and have a good idea where we were going. Anyway, we got the message that they would follow us, using their tail lights to warn other traffic on the road. So, off we set and arrived at the camp without any problems. We still didn't know what the situation would be regarding what action they would take; would they just leave or would they report us to the camp commander? We were lucky, they gave us a big smile, a wave and off they went. We thanked our lucky stars and heaved a big sigh of relief.

The day of testing the guns arrived. It was to be viewed by a number of officers, so they'd set up a viewing point overlooking the range, where the officers could see everything that was taking place. I seem to remember that the armourer had a problem and the exercise had to be put back for a while. He'd just sorted out the problem, when the officers arrived and took their seats, they'd barely had time to settle down, when the guns fired with spectacular results. They were firing at mock tanks lying out on the range, so the exercise was a great success much to the relief of everyone concerned.

One of the good things about this camp was that they had a cinema. So, after working all day and having plenty to do, always keeping busy. As I've said, it was a lovely area and we would spend time looking around the beauty spots. Then when you felt like it, there was always the cinema to fill the night in.

Around the area, they had a lot of displaced persons living in wooden huts with their families. On a Sunday, they would put on a film for them. You would see them walking down to the cinema, dressed in their Sunday best; I'm sure that at that time, this would be their only entertainment. Remember that this was ten years after the war had ended, so whether they ever managed to return to their own countries and their own homes would be very doubtful.

After six weeks, it was time to pack up and head off back to Iserlohn. I look back on my time in Putlos with a great deal of pleasure, with a good billet, nice weather and let's face it – six weeks was a big chunk out of the time that I had left to do.

Going back to Iserlohn, we would be driving a lot on the autobahns (motorways). I don't know if they were all the same but the one we were driving on had a seam across the road at regular intervals. With the result, as you were driving along, you would hear and feel this awful click, which after a while – a very short while I might add – became very annoying. I've been on the continent a few times over the years and have never heard it, so I'm sure like everywhere else, big improvements have taken place.

After getting back to camp and getting settled in, I found I was due to spend a day on the rifle range. This was an activity I didn't mind. I found it quite enjoyable, actually, so I was looking forward to it. There was a lot of competition on the rifle range, with you always wanting to do better than the next man. If you reached a certain score, you would become a marksman and be entitled to wear a badge of crossed rifles on the arm of your B.D. tunic. I was well up for this, as I was quite a good shot and I fancied this badge, unfortunately I just missed out by a few points.

You would also have to take a turn in the target area. This meant that after the rifleman had taken a shot, you would have to pinpoint where he had hit the target, so he could adjust his next shot if need be.

After the firing was finished, the command would be given to unload, after unloading the officer would walk along the line checking everyone's rifle. On this occasion, the officer discovered one of the men still had a bullet in the breach of his gun. To say that the officer went spare would be putting it mildly. He wasn't amused at all and ordered the N.C.O. to put the man on a charge. It was a very dangerous situation – anything to do with firearms has to be treated with the greatest respect.

After that, it was back to the camp and got stuck into the down side of the day. That was the cleaning of the rifle. This is when you renewed your acquaintance with the pull-through and the four-by-two. You would spend ages getting the job done – it had to be right – then of course there was always the inevitable inspection.

CHAPTER THIRTY-ONE

Having spent a bit of time in the camp, we got word that the next exercise was to be held once again on the Sennelager Plains. An area I had become very familiar with over the last twenty months. Only this time, on my return to Iserlohn, I would be very close to my demob date, something that I had been looking forward to for the last two years. Nothing ever seems to go smoothly – there was a problem looming on the horizon. There was growing concern about the situation in the Suez Canal. It was looking very serious and leading us to have some doubts as to whether we would be demobbed on time. It was certainly looking as if the situation could lead to war being declared, so what would happen to us was very much up in the air.

We'd been out on this particular exercise for a few days. It was a big exercise with other regiments involved, and of course, these regiments had R.E.M. E. personnel on the exercise with them. Attached to one of the regiments was a R.E.M.E. sergeant, who was a regular soldier and during his army career must have been on every course the army had ever invented. He was approached by an officer asking him if he had any experience of waterproofing vehicles. Seemingly they were looking for men with this experience to send to the Suez Canal. The sergeant told the officer that he didn't, so the officer asked him if he knew of anyone with this knowledge. The only one that the sergeant could think of was a craftsman attached to the Worcestershire Regiment and proceeded to tell the officer where we were camped.

I can still remember this officer arriving at the camp late at night looking for me, asking if I had any knowledge of the waterproofing of vehicles. That the R.E.M.E. sergeant had told him there was a possibility I could have the knowledge he was looking for. As mentioned before, the reason they were looking for men was because of the situation in the Suez Canal.

Luckily, I was able to tell him I didn't have the experience that he was looking for. I got the impression there would have been no ifs or buts, it would be a case of up and off, and never mind your demob. Of course, at the same time under my breath, I was thanking the sergeant for being so kind as to recommend me in the first place (I don't think I could have seen him far enough).

We got word that one of the vehicles had broken down on the firing range. We had a breakdown truck so one of the craftsmen took a driver and went off to tow it back to where we were camped. They'd been away for a while when an officer turned up asking for the breakdown truck. On telling him that it was away, pulling a truck off the firing range, he said, 'For goodness sake! They're using the range today.'

We jumped into a Champ and set off for the range, we hadn't got very far when we saw the breakdown truck coming towards us. We heaved a big sigh of relief, they did say they'd heard firing but that it had been a way in the distance. Luckily the broken-down truck had been lying to one side of the range, but I must admit my heart was in my mouth until we found them safe and sound.

When we got to the end of the exercise, we packed up and headed off to Iserlohn, for – in my case anyway – the last time. Hopefully, I would get my demob date confirmed and that would be me, I would be off back home and return to normal.

CHAPTER THIRTY-TWO

Eventually the day arrived that it appeared on company orders that I would have to report to the company office. At the office I would find out that my demob date was still the same and to tell me about my travel arrangements. I would be leaving Iserlohn a few days before I was due out and I'd be heading to either Colchester or Aldershot – I've had to put the two names down because one day I think it was Colchester and the next day I'm thinking that it was Aldershot. The *only* thing I'm positive about was that it was definitely one or the other, and this is where I would spend my last few days of my service.

Some time before, the government had decided men doing their national service would be given the opportunity of signing on for an extra year. Before this came about, the minimum you could sign on for was three years. By this time, we had a new M.T.O. One day, I was out with him when he said, 'Why don't you sign on for an extra year? I'm sure you would enjoy it.'

The main reason for him thinking I would enjoy it was because there was a possibility the battalion was to be posted to the West Indies. I'm sure this would have been classed as one of the cream postings in the army, but as tempting as it might have been, the only ambition I had as far as the army was concerned, was to get out and get back home. Whether the Worcesters were ever posted to the West Indies or not I don't know, but I'm sure I was told in good faith.

Nearer the time for me to leave Iserlohn, my name appeared on company orders telling me I had to report to the commanding officer's office at a given time. This was to see the lieutenant-colonel that I've previously mentioned. I knew it was common practice for him to have a word with everyone before they left the battalion, so it was nothing to worry about. At the given time, I reported to his office, to be marched in front of the colonel by the regimental sergeant major, looking my very best, I didn't want to fall foul of him at this stage in the proceedings.

There were two of us on parade so the colonel said he wouldn't ask us if we'd enjoyed our time in the battalion, he just hoped they hadn't been too hard on us. At this everyone laughed, and even the R.S.M. gave a wee grin (maybe my imagination is running away with me).

CHAPTER THIRTY-THREE

The last few days of my time in Iserlohn were spent getting all my gear together preparing for the big day. I've said before that I'd made good friends over the time I'd spent with the Worcesters. But the sadness of leaving was nothing compared to the elation I felt at having come to the end of my time in the army.

The day arrived and I was off to the railway station to board a train and head off across Germany and into Holland (the Netherlands). Arriving in the Hook of Holland, I would board a boat back to the U.K. After leaving the train it seemed a long way, as if you had to walk for miles to get to the boat. It probably wasn't that far but it seemed at the time, especially as I was carrying all my kit. I got to the boat to find that it was still the same system; down into the bowels of the boat, remembering the horrendous journey that I'd experienced on a previous occasion.

Needless to say, my first job was to locate the toilets. After all, it was best to be prepared, but the trip turned out to be quite good with no problems so I landed in Harwich in one piece and feeling fine. On arriving at Colchester or Aldershot, I reported to the guardroom, got booked in and was shown to my quarters. Then given the time that I would have to be on parade the next day.

I got settled and then had a walk around the camp. I was passing this hut when I heard someone shout. It turned out to be a chap that had been in Ellesmere at the same time as me. As the day went on, I met other people I had last seen during my training days in Honiton.

The next few days would be spent handing in equipment that you wouldn't be keeping and to go through the procedure of filling in all the necessary paperwork involved with being demobbed from the army. The funny thing was that the situation in the Suez Canal cropped up again. Luckily not for me, as they were still allowing national servicemen to be demobbed. The situation with Suez was becoming more serious by the day, with the result that all the regular soldiers due to be demobbed were being kept back. Also, they were recalling a large number of reservists, a lot of them based in the same camp as us.

The thing we found amusing about the reservists – although I'm sure they didn't find anything amusing about being recalled to the army – was when the bugler sounded *Sick Parade* there would be men appearing from every direction. I'm not joking, there would be hundreds on *Sick Parade*. I knew how they felt – if I'd have been recalled, I'm sure I would have been on *Sick Parade* as well.

We had to have a medical before we left the army. I say a 'medical', but all I can remember about it was that we all had to stand in a circle with the medical officer standing in the centre. Told to drop our trousers and cough; that was it, I must have passed, I never heard another word about it. One good thing about our time there, was that although we were kept on the move during the day, we got the chance at night to socialise with the people that we had met up with again.

We would get the chance to exchange our experiences of what we had done for the last two years and where we had been. One thing we had in common though, was that we were all pleased it was coming to an end, thinking how lucky we were compared to the regulars and reservists.

Of course, we would still have to check company orders every day; it was a must, you had to make sure your name wasn't on it for some duty or other. Now, I'm sure I could count on one hand the number of times I'd been on guard duty over the two years. On checking, I found on my very last night of my army service I was down for guard duty.

It was a case of getting ready and reporting to the guardroom, and it turned out to be a memorable night. The heavens opened and it absolutely chucked down. One thing I do remember about the camp was standing looking over a high wall, which overlooked the town. It was my last night so I didn't care what the weather was like, that was it.

The next day, I had to catch a train to Newcastle, and once there, I had to make my way to a Territorial Unit. After reporting there, I would be free to make my way home. I got down to Newcastle Central Station to catch a train to Hexham, a journey I had made countless times over the years – but this one was special.

On reaching Hexham, I can still remember walking from the railway station with my kit bag slung over my shoulder and heading for home. I remember one of the sergeants saying to us, 'Get out of your uniform and into civvies as soon as possible.'

Which is what I did. That was it, I was out and that is all that mattered.

I've just said that was me finished, but I was wrong. I would have to report to the Territorial Unit in Hexham. This unit was based at the top of Hencoates, so that is what I did, and this time that was definitely me finished. I still kept my uniform, I often thought over the years at the sign of any trouble, I hope that they don't call me back. I'm pleased to report they never did.

CHAPTER THIRTY-FOUR

Of course, the repercussions of being in the army weren't over. I'd been away for two years and now I was a married man, so what about my job and where would we live? The law was that the firm that was employing you when you went into national service would have to offer you a job when you came out. I had been employed by British Rail, they operated country wide, so I could be offered a job anywhere in the network.

After a few days, I went down to the Greenfield Works in Gateshead, which was where I'd been working prior to joining the army. I knew the office manager well – I'd always got on well with him. He was telling me I'd been allocated a job in Halifax. Now, Halifax was just a name to me, I probably wouldn't know where to look for it on the map. So, I got quite a shock, it looked as if I would be on the move again, something that didn't appeal to me at that time.

We were discussing the situation, when who walks in, but the workshop foreman.

'Oh!' said the office manager. 'You're looking for a mechanic, aren't you? Keith's just out of the army and he's looking for a job.'

'Well yes, I am,' said the foreman, 'but I'm needing someone right away.' He thought about it and asked, 'When can you start?'

So, I said, 'If you can give me a week that would suit me fine.'

'Okay,' said the foreman, 'the job's yours.'

I've often wondered what would have happened if the foreman hadn't walked into the office at that moment. I suppose if I had to go to Halifax, I would have given it a go, but I felt much happier staying in the area.

We were staying with my mother and father at the time, but we were always on the look-out for somewhere to rent. I started work the following week – back to the days prior to national service. Travelling down to Gateshead, catching the early morning train to Newcastle, hopping onto a bus and across to Gateshead.

At night, 5.30 was our finishing time, which meant I wouldn't get home until 7 o'clock. So, I arranged with the foreman that I would leave at 5.10, so I could catch the express train to Hexham and be home at 6 o'clock. Right enough, it was a rush but I managed to catch it most days. We were looking to rent a place nearer to my work when we saw an advert in the paper for a flat in Monkseaton, which was much handier for work and in a nice area – another bonus was that there was an excellent train service.

We went down to view the flat, it turned out to be a couple of rooms with a small kitchen. However, we were quite taken by it, and decided it was for us and we certainly enjoyed the time that we stayed there. I didn't have to be up so early in the morning, which was a bonus, and when I got to Newcastle I had time to walk across the High Level Bridge. This is a combined road and rail bridge, so I enjoyed walking across in the morning and back at night. The trains were very regular so you never had long to wait.

One of the nice things about the flat was that it was just a ten minutes' walk to Whitley Bay, so we would enjoy walking down there, especially at weekends in the summertime.

We were always on the lookout for a house of our own, though. After a few months, we found out we were expecting our first baby, so it was even more important for us to find a place as the flat was on the third floor, which would be far from ideal with a baby to look after.

We had a good look around the area and found out that a new estate was being built just outside Blaydon (I'm sure you will have heard of the song *Blaydon Races*), the name of the estate was Stella Park. We went to have a look at it, some of the houses had already been completed but there were still sites available. We liked what we saw, so we were able to choose the site that we were interested in from the site plan. We were also able to walk up the estate to have a look exactly where the house would be. We put down a deposit, so it was just a case of waiting patiently until the house was completed.

At times, I would have to go to Goods Yard in Blaydon to carry out some work, so I would get the chance to pop along to the estate and see how the house was progressing. One thing I must say is that this was a brand new, three-bedroom house with a good-sized garden and – wait for it – a bay window. All for the princely sum of £1650. I'm looking at this figure and I can hardly believe it, but it's a fact. It just shows how things have changed over the years.

Our oldest son was born in August of 1957 and we moved into the house in November the same year.

We spent three happy years there, spending holidays in Inverness. My wife's mother had died in 1958, so when we did visit Inverness, her father would be asking us to move up there to live with him on the family croft. Eventually that is what we decided to do, moving to Inverness in April of 1961.

In those days, jobs were much easier to find than they are now, so on the first of June – The Glorious First of June – I started working for one of the major oil companies. I must admit that the decision we made to come and live in Inverness and having been here for nearly forty-five years is something I've never regretted.

CHAPTER THIRTY-FIVE

I started this book by writing that some people would like to see the national service return. Every so often the subject appears in the press and on TV, depicting life for national servicemen during the 1950s. Whether the youngsters of today would accept the discipline required by the services are, to say the least, very debatable.

However, I do believe that given time the officers and N.C.O.s would get the message across and they would begin to enjoy it. But whether national service is the answer in my opinion is highly unlikely. I'm afraid that the answer to discipline with youngsters lies long before their eighteenth birthday. As far as I'm concerned, my two years in the army didn't do me any harm. I looked on it as something that I had to do and I'm sure the experience broadened my horizons.

You had to take the rough with the smooth, but at times I quite enjoyed it. It wasn't a total waste of time for the over two million men who served during the time that national service was in force. I'm sure every one of them has their own memories of the good times and the bad, and certainly of the occasions they wouldn't like to see in print.

So here ends the story of the reluctant soldier and his two years out.

I hope that you enjoy reading it as much as I've enjoyed writing it. I have never kept a diary so these recollections are how I remember times long past.

ABOUT THE AUTHOR

Keith Irving, born in 1933 in the North of England, has carved a fulfilling life journey. After pursuing an engineering apprenticeship in Hexham, he temporarily delayed his national service commitment. At the age of twenty-one, Keith embarked on his national service, serving two years with the Royal Electrical and Mechanical Engineers in Germany. Keith continued his engineering career and eventually settled in Inverness, Scotland, with his wife Margaret, whom he has been married to for nearly seventy years. They, along with their two sons, continued the family croft on the picturesque shores of Loch Ness. Fondly known as "Grandda Sheep" by his grandchildren, Keith and Margaret also ran a thriving Bed and Breakfast for several decades, delighting visitors with their warm hospitality.

Keith's thirst for exploration extended far beyond his national service days. He embarked on numerous adventures, traversing six continents and witnessing the beauty of diverse cultures and landscapes. Now in retirement, Keith finds joy in his hobbies, such as avidly watching game shows, indulging in daily biking sessions covering five miles on his exercise bike, and pursuing his passion for bowling.

However, Keith's greatest satisfaction comes from observing the lives of his children, grandchildren, and great-grandchild as they carry forward his legacy of love for Scotland, learning, travel, football, and family history. Throughout the years, he has fostered a safe and supportive environment for his loved ones, earning their deep affection and respect.

Keith Irving's life is a testament to the power of family, the pursuit of knowledge and adventure, and the ability to find contentment in the simple joys of life. Secretly, if he had another go at life, he would have tried his hand (or voice) at a singing career.

Printed in Great Britain
by Amazon

26552813R00106